SISTER TO SISTER: TO KNOW I AM

by

Linda McGinnis & Diane McGinnis

Copyright © 2011 Linda Davis & Diane L. Turner

All rights reserved.

ISBN: ISBN-13: 978-1456453770
ISBN-10: 1456453777

CONTENTS

FORWARD

This devotional is a unique collection of correspondence between two sisters who sought to encourage one another in the faith. Sisters can be a source of strength to each other, like mountains that rise against the skyline in beauty. With words of wisdom and comfort, sisters in the Lord can minister to one another, sharing insights learned at our Father's feet.

Our motivation in writing this collection of verse and thoughts was to help each other go deeper in our relationship with Christ, and beyond that, to extend these encouragements to all of our sisters in the body of Christ.

We wrote to each other as the Lord began to show us things about himself in nature and in the simple things of life, as well as through characters and stories of the Bible. We shared these ideas with one other, sending countless letters of verse and thoughts through the mail between our respective homes in New York and Maryland. The sister who wrote the particular verse illustrating a facet of the "I Am" also penned the devotional thoughts, and then the other sister would answer with a prayer response, so that each devotion is a composite of the two sisters working together to express a fullness of the original idea.

As you read, you might begin to notice the two differing styles, indicative of the two different, yet related personalities. As sisters, we share mannerisms, looks, and many thoughts. We differ, however, in the way we express ourselves and use language to communicate. We hope you will enjoy the interplay of our thoughts and ideas as we learned from each other and inspired one another from week to week. We hope this book is a blessing to all our "sisters" in the faith.

–Linda McGinnis

The sum of all we know about God could be condensed into this brief phrase: He is. "I Am that I Am," he says about himself. This knowledge gives the peace passing all understanding. How can we meet and experience God? We know he is a God that wants to be known by his people.

By his grace, God continually sparks our awareness of himself. He reveals himself to us, sometimes openly, often in secret. As light sparkles in a prism, our understanding of him is beautiful and colorful. But just as certain types of light are hidden to the naked eye, so too our spiritual eyes are blind to some aspects of the "I Am". We cannot contain God in our finite minds. We respond in awe and are intrigued by the secrets of God.

Let's go now into the secret place. Let us be still. Let us discover the Great "I Am".

–Diane McGinnis

An Invitation –

Anyone can know Jesus, the Great I AM. If you would like to have a personal relationship with Christ, he invites you to open your heart and receive him as Lord and Savior. He died on the cross to save your soul and forgive your sins. He offers the promise of new life now, and eternal life with him forever in heaven.

All Scripture quotations, unless otherwise indicated, are taken from the HOLY BIBLE, NEW INTERNATIONAL VERSION . NIV . Copyright 1973, 1978,1984 by the International Bible Society. Used by permission of Zondervan Publishing House. All rights reserved.

1
NATURE

"Does not the very nature of things teach you…"
1 Corinthians 11:14

MUSIC

"Even the sparrow has found a home, and the swallow a nest for herself, where she may have her young- a place near your altar, O Lord Almighty, my King and my God. Blessed are those who dwell in your house; they are ever praising you."
Psalm 84:3,4

Sparrow for a penny sold
Many more, your worth is told
Ravens in the wood will fly
No barn or storeroom keeps them dry.

Fed by God, they worry not,
Nor one of them will be forgot
The birds have found a place to dwell
Upon the altar, songs will swell.

Praising Him with one accord
Delighting in abiding Lord.
Like music from the waking birds,
To know I Am, you must be heard.

Dear Sister,

How we can revel in the birdsong that comes with the morning sun! Each day a different combination of trills and warbles greets our ears, with a vast array of notes both high and low. How pleasant it is to find a resting place near the altar of the Most High to declare our praises. We join with a multitude of voices, from each resounds the glories and marvels of our Father in heaven. In such a sheltered place, full of the sounds of joy, we would never grow tired of the ongoing symphony and refrain. Let your voice join with others, raise up a melody to extol our Maker. This, of all pastimes, brings us closest to our heavenly occupation, for will not the multitudes of heaven produce a sound so lovely and loud it resembles the roaring of a waterfall and the loudest peals of thunder? For now, the music of our praise must be uttered in the realm of this earth. How we rejoice in preparation for the day when our praises will join the mighty throng of worshipers that populate the heavenly city! For now, sing loud, sing long, sing to him, and be assured it is a beautiful sound in the ears of your God.

A Prayer

Lord, I will open my mouth to praise you. I will worship at your altar. May I sing a new song unto you, may I sing a song that is beautiful to your ears. You inhabit the praises of your people, so help me to worship you in spirit and in truth.

MORNING SUN

"In the heavens he has pitched a tent for the sun, which is like a bridegroom coming forth from his pavilion, like a champion rejoicing to run his course. It rises at one end of the heavens and makes its circuit to the other; nothing is hidden from its heat."
Psalm 19:4-6

Rising in the eastern gate,
The solar wind that penetrates
With a bridegroom's heady force
Like mighty man upon his course,

Yellow, red, and orange fire
Casting light that never tires,
Faithful as a morning song
Piercing sun to earth belongs.

Beaming from the purest skies,
Filling up my open eyes,
Like a diamond beyond worth,
To know I Am, you must shine forth.

Dear Sister,

Every morning without fail, the sun rises and blazes over the earth, giving warmth and light. In a multitude of households the beams and rays invade the darkness through windows and doors, and shout the news, a new day has arrived! Day after day, turning into months and years, centuries and millenniums, the sun has shone without fail. How like the symbolic shining of our lives, going forth into the dark corners of the earth, shedding beams of God's compassion upon the cracks and crevices of desolate humanity. How he inspires us, the Light of the World, to shine as he does, to let the flame he has kindled in our hearts be cast upon his creation. The darkest of nights, heavy laden with troubles and despair, must be dispelled at the dawn. Once again the sun rises above the horizon in its glory and splendor. What light God gives us in this tireless sun, magnificent in its burning! Even from behind the clouds, beams and rays find release, and spray heavenly encouragement upon the land. With the light God has given us, may we shine forth a dazzling display for the lost and hurting. May we light a path that leads them to bow at his feet.

A Prayer

I will not hide my light under a bushel! Give me boldness, Father, to shine forth with your beauty and splendor. Let all darkness and shadows flee away, let me be a beacon to the lost and the hurting. Your light is strong and unwavering. Give me a candle that goes not out by night.

THE SPRING

"Therefore, if anyone is in Christ, he is a new creation; the old has gone, the new has come!"
2 Corinthians 5:17

Lengthened days, a warmer sun,
Calls to nature, Winter's done
The geese return, the robin's seen,
The air becomes so fresh and clean.

A flower poking through the ground
Long and green, it once was round
And hard, resembled not
The shape and sight that it begot.

Buds wrapped tightly on a tree
Hold a promise what's to be.
Like water makes both snow and rain,
To know I Am, you must be changed.

Dear Sister,

We must awaken our soul, for it is spring. If we listen, we can hear his cry: "Rise up, my love, my fair one, and come away! The winter is past! The rain is over and gone."(KJV) It is a season of love and grace for us, if we will enter into his kingdom. He has promised to take us from glory to glory, and if we look toward heaven, we will be transformed. Just as a tender bulb responds to the warmth of sun and generous rains in the spring, our hearts will respond to his compassion and loving kindness. We will be changed. Our minds will be renewed, our face will shine with the oil of gladness, and our hearts of stone will be exchanged for hearts of flesh. He has also given us a new name. What newness of life! What glorious resurrection! When he has changed us we will hear him say, "Thou art fair, my love; there is no spot in thee."

A Prayer

Lord, I want to be changed. I will look heavenward and be changed into your image. I will let the light of your Son fall upon me, and the rains of your refreshing touch my soul. Let spring come into my heart, a new season of hope and promise. I am ready!

THE STORM

"Therefore everyone who hears these words of mine and puts them into practice is like a wise man who built his house on the rock. The rain came down, the streams rose, and the winds blew and beat against that house; yet it did not fall, because it had its foundation on the rock."
Matthew 7:24,25

Thunder rages, lightning flash,
Rain in waves falls down to dash
Wind, relentless, swells and sways
Pounding drops and cloud displays,

Bending limbs, a roaring comes,
Silence, then a burst of drums
Such crescendo and a crash
Sweeping down, the noises clash,

The house, it shakes and cracks appear,
The soul, it quakes and suffers fear
Like rock erodes, but keeps its form,
To know I Am, you face the storm.

Dear Sister,

Oh, the fury of a thunderstorm! It never ceases to
fascinate us in its magnitude and consequence. A combination
of forces, nature at her strongest, beats against the structures
and buildings of men. Will they stand? Are they strong enough?
Will the next storm be stronger, fiercer, more powerful than
the last? How important it is for us to build on the rock. Many
times we think that is what we are doing, and we busy ourselves
with our construction. It might look like a fine work, artistic,
functional, having all the appearance of sturdiness and strength.
It is not until the test comes that we can be sure of its
soundness. And the test will come. It is God's mercy at work
when he sometimes allows the storms of life to expose the
cracks in our spiritual houses. God's mercy, because it is better
to be aware of the state of your soul, than to be deluded about
what you are made of. What fleeting things we put our time
and efforts into while we traverse this earth! May God give us
the courage to face each storm, the grace to rebuild when we
have suffered damages, and the eyes to see the task which has
its origins in him. Our rubble and debris will be swept away,
but the house built on him will stand secure.

A Prayer

Lord of the thunder and the storm, I will not fear. You are with
me. I know there is no flood which could overtake me. The
forces that assail me are strong, but will lead me to the rock
that is higher than I. In you I can face the storm.

BLAZING COMET

*"The heavens declare the glory of God; the skies proclaim the
work of his hands. Day after day they pour forth speech; night
after night they display knowledge. There is no speech or
language where their voice is not heard."*
Psalm 19:1,2

Blazing comet, late at night
A stunning spectacle of light
I look, I gaze, and I admire
This hurling ball of smoke and fire.

Who could create space and time
And decorate it so sublime?
If earth and moon is where we live
Who could have such gifts to give?

Someone bigger than a man
Chance could not, it is too grand
When your eyes behold and see,
To know I Am, you must believe.

Dear Sister,

In the darkest of nights, God's creation sparkles with fantastic beauty. All men live and breathe under the same sky. It is not reserved for the rich, the wise, or the chosen. It is alive, it shines and radiates for all to see. Who will look up? Each solar body, each planet, star, and mass sends forth and reflects light which races towards us with tremendous speed. And for every man who stands peering out into the night sky from his corner of the earth there is a testimony that speaks. We see a picture of God's righteousness, so many times greater and brighter than ourselves, shining down upon our unsuspecting souls and giving us hope in our darkness. Who is great enough to bring this perfect righteousness near, to tell us his salvation is not far off? Lift up your eyes and see! Who created it all? Our meditation leads us to God. If we think upon just one of these celestial bodies, its massive size, its powerful energy, and its great speed, we can hardly fathom it. He calls them all by name. He spun them into existence off the tips of his fingers. He places them and orders them and holds them all together. We are convinced by reason of the grand universe and its testimony that God is real. We are sure that he is. And his words echo back at us: "I Am."

A Prayer

The work of your hands, Lord, is awesome and spectacular. You are an artist beyond compare. I will look up and behold the grand universe you have made. I will listen to the voice of your beautifully decorated heavens. I will admire it all, and worship you, my Creator.

Linda McGinnis & Diane McGinnis

2
LIFE

"In the beginning was the Word…"
John 1:1

IN THE SECRET PLACE

*"Now the earth was formless and empty, darkness was
over the surface of the deep, and the Spirit of God was hovering
over the waters. And God said, 'Let there be light,' and there
was light." Genesis 1:2,3*

Inside the lifeless, darkness deep
Lies now a child, fast asleep
Without resist, without protest,
The Father creates, the child rests.

First there is silence, then a sound,
The voice of God, his love surrounds,
And speaks his thoughts to sweetest rose,
The child is in such repose.

There is much to this design,
Perfection comes in these months nine,
A picture of the Father's will,
To know I am, you must be still.

Dear Sister,

It is inside the hidden places, the voids, and the darkness that the Spirit of God begins to move. We do not see all he does, just as we do not see all he is. Our awareness of God is limited, for he is so much more than we can comprehend. We experience the goodness of God when we cease from our works, when we enter into rest. King David spoke of the womb as the secret place, and such knowledge was too wonderful for him. We do not see the Almighty create in the secret place. When God questioned Job about where he was when the foundations of the earth were laid, he responded by putting his hand upon his mouth. We must be silent as he reveals himself, and creates. Adam was in a deep sleep when Eve was formed. So too we sleep, and he goes about his work. We begin our journey as a child in the womb, in the dark, where we have no ability to claim understanding. In the deepest of waters, the darkest place, there the Spirit of God will move. There the Father is ready to declare, "Let there be light!"

A Prayer

Lord, I will be still and let you work. Create in me beauty and life. I will not protest or resist your careful hand. Help me to remain silent, and hear your loving voice. I want to enter into your rest, and enjoy with you the things you have created. Bring the light of understanding into my heart!

LESSONS OF THE BIRTH

"I tell you the truth, no one can see the kingdom of God unless
he is born again."
John 3:3

From within the womb a start,
A pressure builds, the Father's art
Anticipates, without delay
A launching to the light of day.

A call, a voice, enticing song,
Will draw the ready child along
Encouraged, seed will shoot, believe
Unhurried, yet compelled to leave.

Bursting forth in seconds few
In naked beauty, pure and true
As light upon a cloudless morn,
To know I Am, you must be born.

Dear Sister,

There is a sure thing in this life, if a man is born he will one day die. This life has the potential to be wonderful, if we will only be "born again." Like the moment of our entrance into this world, a spiritual birth takes place in an instant, a journey whereby the spirit is awakened and we are launched into the kingdom of God, a new and unknown experience. Just as the babe in the womb is compelled to exit the place of its conception, the seed of the word of God in our hearts germinates and shoots above the earth to be seen by men. It is a glorious awakening, this moment when our eyes come into the light, when new sights are forced upon us suddenly, when all the familiar becomes unfamiliar, and yet we are glad. Something beautiful and pure is revealed to the eye present at the birthing, the one who stands aside to see this miracle. Necessary, desired and awaited with much anticipation, the birth leads us into a walk with the great "I Am", a journey that cannot begin without its occurrence, a journey in fact, that will have no end.

A Prayer

I celebrate new life, the new life in me, and the new life I see in others. You alone, Father, create this life, and in you I will rejoice and be glad. Let us love and treat with tenderness all those who are babes in you. Let us see in their beauty your beauty, and let us see in their smile a reflection of your face!

FIRST BREATH

"I am the Lord your God, who brought you up out of Egypt.
Open wide your mouth and I will fill it."
Psalm 81:10

Arriving wrinkled, wet, and blue
What can sustain a life so new?
Without knowing what is done
The Father's breath fills his lung.

Out comes a cry, a piercing yell
A voice to sound out loud and well
For now the child breathes to weep,
But later he will learn to speak

In the first moment of his birth,
The waking breath has so much worth
Like blast of wind upon a hill,
To know I Am, you must be filled.

Dear Sister,

There is nothing quite like the excitement of a newborn's first breath. There is a gasp as oxygen enters his lungs for the first time. His chest expands, he is filled! Such a blast of air is necessary to his life, and will sustain him as long as he lives. When man was formed in the garden, God breathed upon him the breath of life. A Holy moment! After his resurrection, Jesus also breathed on his disciples, signifying a new beginning for them as they followed him. Just as a child needs air to breathe, so also we need the Holy Spirit in our spiritual lives. In him we have boldness, comfort, and joy. When we are baptized in the Holy Spirit, it is like a child taking his first breath. But there is more to breathing than the first breath, and we must be continually filled with the Holy Spirit in our daily walk. He has promised that when we ask according to his will, we shall receive, and he loves to give good gifts to his children. Will you ask for the Holy Spirit? It is his joy to fill you!

A Prayer

Lord, fill me with the breath of life, your wondrous Holy Spirit. Let the breath of God bring life to my dead bones, let it revive and refresh my soul. I need it each moment of every day, and I depend on you to fill me with yourself. Fill me until my cup overflows.

CRADLE OF LIFE

"Can a mother forget the baby at her breast and have no compassion on the child she has borne? Though she may forget, I will not forget you! See, I have engraved you on the palms of my hands; your walls are ever before me."
Isaiah 49:15,16

Suspended, filled with life, apart
Newborn reaches out to balance heart
Without cradle, without bed
Father show a place to lay the head

Voice of comfort, light as feather spoken
Mother's breast, receiving token,
From above, cherishing this one
Stability gives, like warmth with rising sun.

A perfect fit, cradle of the mother's arms
Babe is safe, secure and warm,
Graven on the Father's hand to meld,
To know I Am, you must be held.

Dear Sister,

Oh, the security of being consoled in our mother's arms! No child outgrows this need, and most mothers reluctantly yield up the practice when size prevents it. Yet we have the Father's promise to continually hold us in his arms. Carved upon his hands, we are part of him, we are joined to him, never to be forgotten. Who has not seen the crying infant, when returned to his mother, nestle firmly against her heart and cease his protestations? This comforting place gives balance not only to an infant, but to young children of most any age, and who has not found the need for a reassuring hug even as an adult? It is a sign that between a mother and her child there are no walls, no hindrances, no limited access, but an allowance for the warmth necessary to grow up with a sense of being loved. We are admonished to be like children as we approach the Father, to trust him with our whole hearts. How hard should this be, when he provides us a sure haven, the very cradle of his hands, held out to bear us continually? We must allow it, we must take our comfort from the stability he is ready to provide. We must not shrink away from the closeness of being loved by him in this encompassing way. Between us and our God, no wall, no hindrance, and no hurt is too large to be overcome by his entreaty, "I have engraved you upon my hands." He tells us it is done.

A Prayer

Thank you dear Father, for your strong and inseparable hold upon us. I find comfort and refuge in your everlasting arms. I know wherever I go, whatever I do, you are caring for me. Nothing shall separate us. I shall rest in the cradle of your arms.

DRINK OF LIFE

"I tell you the truth, unless you eat the flesh of the Son of Man
and drink his blood, you have no life in you. Whoever eats my
flesh and drinks my blood has eternal life, and I will raise him
up at the last day. For my flesh is real food, and my blood is
real drink. Whoever eats my flesh and drinks my blood remains
in me, and I in him."
John 6:53-56

A pang within the belly rises up
The mouth of babe will search for earthly cup
Without words and cord to give
Supply, he must now eat to live.

A drop of milk upon his cheek
From mother's source to fill his weak
And feeble form, he makes the link
Like root that draws from earth to drink.

A nourishment so perfect and refined
If only for a season and a time
As drops of blood from Christ were shed,
To know I Am, you must be fed.

Dear Sister,

Physical nourishment consists of food for the belly, while the body and blood of Christ is the nourishing sustenance for the spirit. These words of Christ are hard to understand, and yet no one would deny the requirement for a babe to feed at mother's breast. This babe is dependant for the sustenance that will enable him to grow into a healthy child. He must be fed, and it is the responsibility of another to see he gets what he needs. Even so, our Father gives us our daily bread. And what does he give for our spiritual needs? He gives himself. No less than his flesh, broken for us, and his blood shed at Calvary. We should partake, and so enjoy the privilege of remaining in him. He feeds us food appropriate for our stage in growth, increasing the amount as we expand our hearts in receiving it. Just as the children of Israel received their daily manna, let us receive the true bread from heaven, as Jesus told us he was. This is the bread that will sustain our weak and feeble forms, bread to make us strong in the faith. And yet, we remain dependant, each day needing fresh manna, looking to his throne for our supply. Let us be linked to the source of our nourishment, and trust him for the food which gives us life.

A Prayer

Lord, I do hunger and thirst for your righteousness. And what a banquet you have provided! I will partake of this heavenly food. I know it is all I need. I will draw near and take the sincere milk you give. In you is the fountain of life.

A QUIET PLACE

"Come to me, all you who are weary and burdened, and I will give you rest." Matthew 11:28

"Find rest, O my soul, in God alone; my hope comes from him." Psalm 62:5

Little baby, so new to life
Unfamiliar sounds and sights
Do press, and crowd your little bed,
Do come close, and lay your head.

I'll hold you, I will calm your fears
The toil and the noise you hear,
Will fade when you are in my arms,
I'll keep you far away from harm

My beloved, I give you sleep
For I'm the Good Shepherd of the sheep
Like John who leaned upon my breast,
To know I Am, you too must rest.

Dear Sister,

Rest is something we all need, but it is especially important to babies. They are continually adapting to a brand new way of life. They often cry when they are tired. It is beautiful to see a baby being picked up and placed in the arms of its mother. This place of comfort is pleasing to an infant. Feeling safe and warm, the child drifts into a much needed sleep. John found a place of refuge, for on the night of the Last Supper, he leaned upon Christ's breast. How beautiful a sight this must have been. Amidst the troubling talk of betrayal, John received comfort in the shadow of the Almighty. No matter what surrounds, if you desire rest, there is one sure source. Christ. Lean on him.

A Prayer

I will rest beneath the shadow of the Almighty. I will lean my weary head upon my Savior, as John did. There is no place I'd rather spend my life, than covered by his everlasting arms. Thank you, Lord, that your arms are stretched out, that you provide a resting place.

SMALL BEGINNIGS

"Let me live that I may praise you, and may your laws sustain me." Psalm 119:175

Man and woman intertwined,
As two meet, the plan divine
Begins, despise not the start
God has joined, don't break apart.

A human being, a special life,
Never meant to know a knife
Of destruction, for out of the mouth of babes
And sucklings, he perfected praise.

In the beginning was the Word
Their silent cries he has heard,
In the womb the Lord doth fill,
To know I Am, you must not kill.

Dear Sister,

This commandment speaks especially to women, for it is from a woman's womb that human life springs forth. Like a seed that is planted and takes root, acceptance for a child begins in the soft refuge of a womb. Not by our choice, but by our natural design, we begin caring for this new life. As simply as we breathe, the child breathes within us. As simply as our hearts beat, the child's also beats within us. As our offspring cling to us, our bodies reach out and give the required nourishment. Mother and child are bonded together. Who has joined them together? Has not God? Therefore, let not man put asunder! He calls his creation good, and gives every good and perfect gift. He has promised to perform the good work he has begun in us until the day of Jesus Christ. He has promised to gently lead those with young. Who has the keys of hell and death? Certainly not a woman. It is the Father of Lights, in whom there is no shadow of turning. Choose, and choose well what you do with small beginnings. The angels, the saints, and the Lord himself are for choice, in this sense only: Choose you this day whom you will serve!

A Prayer

Lord, I will choose life! Life for myself, for my children, for those who have no voice to speak. Help me to uphold the sanctity of life in every situation, to be a voice in defense of the unborn. When I have the opportunity, let my voice join with the multitude of heaven; "Let the unborn children live!"

3
OBEDIENCE

"To obey is better than sacrifice…"
1 Samuel 15:22

BUILD A BOAT

"Noah was a righteous man, blameless among the people of his time, and he walked with God."
Genesis 6:9

"Noah did everything just as God commanded him."
Genesis 6:22

Two by two, the beasts arrived
And Noah took them, satisfied,
Upon the Ark his hands had built
They entered calmly, ordered, filled

Until the day the floodgates poured,
And God himself did shut the door
The waters rose and Ark was born
And tossed upon the mountain's horn

Until at last the outpour ceased,
And dove returned with olive leaf,
The rainbow arc 'd from sky to land
To know I Am, you build as planned.

Dear Sister,

How important it is to follow the instructions the Lord gives us. For the Ark, God gave specific dimensions, telling Noah the exact size to build it, the number of decks to include, and even where to place the door. Noah listened to the plans, and built the Ark accordingly. It was a structure built to withstand the ravages of a flood beyond anything seen up until that time, or since. Did Noah get nervous when the water began to rise and lifted the boat for the first time? Did he think about all the corners he had cut to save time or money in the construction? Gladly, he did not. He knew he had followed the instructions exactly. We should follow his example. We do not build Arks, thankfully, but we do build our lives, relationships, and works that bring God glory. He is ready with the plans, and doesn't require us to figure it all out by chance and guesswork. He gave David and Solomon the plans for the Temple, down to the minutest detail. Will he do less for us? Allow him to teach and instruct you, he knows the best and most efficient way to carry out the commands of God. Will you make time to listen to his plans? Time spent thus is never wasted.

A Prayer

Lord, the plans you have given me are plans for good, to give me a future and a hope. Let me study this plan, hold to this plan, and follow it to the smallest detail. If I trust in your unsearchable wisdom, I will not be ashamed at the end result. Help me build, exactly as you command.

ILLUMINATION

"Some time later, God tested Abraham. He said to him,
'Abraham!' 'Here am I, he replied.'
Then God said, 'Take your son, your only son Isaac, whom you
love, and go to the region of Moriah. Sacrifice him there as a
burnt offering on one of the mountains I will tell you about.'"
Genesis 22:1,2

Strange request from the faultless throne,
A donkey is saddled, wood is hewn,
Fire carried, knife at the waist,
Father, son, Moriah the place

Where, Oh Father, is the lamb
For sacrifice to Great I Am?
He will provide of this I'm sure,
And arm in arm they did endure

The altar set, the wood arranged,
A son is bound, the knife upraised
As lightning flash precede the thunder's force,
To know I Am, you must hear His voice.

Dear Sister,

What consternation Abraham must have felt when the voice of God brought this unusual request! But Abraham had faith, faith that God was capable of raising his son from the dead, and so he made the preparations and went to the mountain. What did God show him there? Did Abraham have a preview of Calvary while his son, his only son, lay upon the altar, and his knife was raised to slay him? And yet, the voice from heaven called out to him, to stop him, directing him to slay a ram in the thicket instead. Abraham had an ear turned to heaven in everything he did. He didn't have the written word, as we do, but had to rely on the spoken word of God. God's revelation comes in many ways, a picture filling our mind, a scripture passage, a sense of the right thing to do. It is up to us to tune our ear, to be aware of the heavenly voice speaking to us, to trust him when he tests us. He will reveal to us mysteries beyond the confines of our own space and time, just as Abraham was granted a vision of the cross, which lay many centuries beyond the short span of his life. The depths of God can never be searched out, but may we have eyes to see the illuminating visions he would show us about himself.

A Prayer

Lord, I desire a pure heart so that I might see you. Illuminate your word, that I might discover who you really are. Open my eyes that I may know more of you. Teach me your ways, that I might walk in them.

FLEE

"Flee from sexual immorality. All other sins a man commits are outside his body, but he who sins sexually sins against his own body. Do you not know that your body is a temple of the Holy Spirit, who is in you, whom you have received from God? You are not your own; you were bought at a price."
1 Corinthians 6:18-20

A well built and a handsome man
Advancing in the Pharaoh's land
Going in and out, in charge,
Prospering, with duties large,

Noticed by the Master's wife
Persistent, lustful, bringing strife,
Luring him to share her couch
But he refused to look or touch

With cunning she reversed the roles,
Revenge, he went to prison hole,
As fuel fed fire can't abate,
To know I Am, don't fornicate.

Dear Sister,

What charms were held out to Joseph, an upright and God fearing man! He shows us the way to resist, although the price he paid was unjust and undeserved. Plagued day in and day out by a woman who sought to implicate him in betrayal, he stood firmly against her attempts to seduce him, convinced that it would be a sin not only against his master, but against God. We, also, should flee youthful lusts and pursue the course that leads to righteousness, faith, love, and peace. Let us determine beforehand that indeed, we have been bought with a great price, and our bodies belong to God. We are no longer free to indulge in sinful pleasures and lust, but we are encouraged to walk in the Spirit. In such a state we will not fulfill the desires of the flesh. Let us strive to walk daily in the Spirit of God, not with pride in our ability to stand, for pride precedes a fall. Rather, we must exhibit a humble state of mind, aware of the pitfalls around us, aware of our weaknesses and frailties, learning to avoid situations and places that will lure us away from a walk with Christ. We must become wise in recognizing the traps of the enemy, and depend on the Holy Spirit to strengthen our resolve to live a life of purity, both in our thoughts, and in our deeds.

A Prayer

Father, I have been bought with a price, and my body is not my own. Though temptation comes persistently, and persuasively, let me not be taken in. I know it would be a sin against you. Help me to guard my heart. Watch over my thoughts, to keep them pure.

A SCARLET WOMAN

"By faith the prostitute Rahab, because she welcomed the spies,
was not killed with those who were disobedient."
Hebrews 11:31

Harlot woman, dressed in red
Had made a fortune in her bed
But then, in virtue, laid some flax,
Upon the roof, on two men's backs.

Her act of faith had made it clear,
Of God, not men, she had true fear,
She let the scarlet rope to fall,
To save her family, one and all.

A sinner, yes, but used of God
Her faith wrought works that we can laud,
As man who built on rock was safe,
To know I Am, you must have faith.

Dear Sister,

Without faith it is impossible to please God. Rahab moved in faith when she hid the spies, a courageous act. We are familiar with the heroes of faith listed in Hebrews. But what about our faith? Is it strong enough to move mountains? Is it small, like a tiny grain of a mustard seed? Don't be discouraged. Remember what God has said about even a small amount of faith. Faith is a gift, it is distributed by God. Use the faith that has been entrusted to you. Believe as much as you are able, and then cry out to God, "Lord, help thou my unbelief!" As the man who brought his child to Christ for deliverance, you may find your faith insufficient. But Christ is sufficient. He can give you faith in greater measure. Whatever you do, perish not in unbelief. Rahab's faith caused her to receive the spies with peace. What is it that your faith will cause you to do today?

A Prayer

Lord, increase my faith. I would believe and do exploits for you, if only you strengthen my faith. Sometimes I feel weak, and my trust falters, but you are able to keep me from falling, able to reaffirm in my heart all you have taught me. I will dwell in your Word, and build up my faith by hearing about the actions of men and women who have gone out on a limb with only faith to sustain them. Thank you for your promises. Make me a woman strong in faith.

LESSONS OF THE LITTLE CHILD

"The Lord was with Samuel as he grew up, and he let none of his words fall to the ground."
1 Samuel 3:19

"Samuel did what the Lord said."
1 Samuel 16:4

Samuel, little chosen child
With chubby face all meek and mild
Without guile, without blame
Responding heart to Father's claim.

A name in the night, an address
An appointment and a test
Of words that speak and must be spoken
As stem begins to firm, and not be broken.

Obedience, the Father's bidding done
Step by step, and one by one
As snow filled mountain stream is fed,
To know I Am, you must be led.

Dear Sister,

Precept upon precept, and line upon line, we grow through childhood to maturity. Each little step of progress and obedience marks the path to wisdom and experience. Samuel was given into the Lord's service at a young age, and listened well to the instruction that came to him from the Lord. How God longs for us to have responding hearts like Samuel did! It is not enough to say we have heard God's voice in the night, but we must ask ourselves, have we obeyed the words he has spoken to us? We go no further in our walk with him when disobedience lies before us, staring us in the face. We are uncomfortable until we carry out the messages and duties the Spirit gives us. Sometimes his voice comes to draw us near in fellowship, at other times to help us adjust our attitudes. How blessed is the man who is led by God, whose steps are ordered by the Almighty, whose hand is held in the grip of heaven. He shall prosper, and see many lives touched by his obedience. We should avoid the pitfall of filling up our lives with things we assume are right, without letting God deal with us specifically in the areas he claims lordship over. Let us, like the stream, follow the path to peace, knowing that if we do we shall hear the promised words, "Well, done, thou good and faithful servant." It is done one step at a time.

A Prayer

I thank you, Lord, for every day you have given me to learn godly truths. They are precious to me. Each one of them leads to more insight, more knowledge, and more understanding of you. Thank you for giving me your word, and teaching me, step by step, how to live it.

A MASTER PLAN

"Let us then approach the throne of grace with confidence, so that we may receive mercy and find grace to help us in our time of need." Hebrews 4:16

A beautiful and gracious maid
Chosen Queen, an honor paid
Decree was signed to threaten life
But God could spare, and they would fight

Evil Haman's anger stewed,
He built the gallows for the Jew,
Esther spoke as Mordecai said,
The wicked Haman died instead.

Such a time as this did prove
God's hand is over all that moves
As scepter reached and grace did bring
To know I Am, you face the King.

Dear Sister,

When we come before the King of Kings with a need or a request, he will hold out his scepter of grace to us. For he is a great king, he knows our needs before we ask. Unlike the king in Esther's day, our Lord can never be tricked into a decree which would cause us harm. His wisdom is unsearchable, his knowledge, complete. He has sovereign control over every earthly event, promising to work all things towards good for them that love him. He uses the elements, as well as men both powerful and weak, to promote his master plan. Look at the stories of Daniel, Joseph, or David. Isn't his faithfulness evident? Every adversity, every unfortunate event was turned around and used for these men's good. Think about where God has you. Ask him to show you his grace. Come to him in every situation. You can have boldness in your time of need before the throne of grace. His love will be stretched out to you as you come. Do not fear, for our King has promised us that those who come to him, he will in no way cast out. Approach the throne, and receive his scepter of grace today.

A Prayer

Lord I desire to approach the throne of grace. Like Esther, I tremble and fast, putting on the garments you have given me, ones appropriate for your throne room. How my heart sings with joy when you receive me, allowing me access to your holy place. What honor is mine as I receive your favor, and I bow my knee with a heart full of thanksgiving.

A QUEST

"My purpose is that they may be encouraged in heart and united in love, so that they may have the full riches of complete understanding, in order that they may know the mystery of God, namely, Christ, in whom are hidden all the treasures of wisdom and knowledge." Colossians 2:2,3

Hearing Rumors in the east,
Traveled far on searching quest
A caravan of spice and gems
A Queen befit with diadems

Arriving with a pressing task
A test of questions she must ask
To wisest man on face of earth
They met and at great length conversed

So much explained, her heart impressed
By palace and his mind expressed
As thoughts surpassed by richest proof
To know I Am, you must seek truth.

Dear Sister,

There can be no encouragement to seek truth, unless we clarify where truth is to be found. Hidden in Christ, waiting to be discovered, truth in its essence awaits the seeking heart. The Queen of Sheba considered Solomon a great marvel, but as we know, a greater than Solomon is here. Bits and pieces of truth can be gleaned from life, from the beauties of nature, from the world around us, but they stand in need of interpretation. We need the understanding that comes from being hid in Christ. We might know the facts, approaching truth as a science, but do we know the reason for our existence? Can we fathom the "why" that explains the truth, can we verbalize it in terms that are understood? There can be no real truth without the acknowledgment of the one who is Truth. Without seeing him as the epitome, truth is only an empty shell whose definition eludes us. The simplest of persons, when in right relationship to the Savior, becomes wiser beyond the seers of this world. Shepherds, fishermen, the lowly, meek, and mild who bow the knee to Christ become filled with wisdom beyond their ability and understanding beyond their experience. Seek him earnestly, for those who seek will find, and in finding him, you will find the wisdom and truth that surpasses earthly knowledge.

A Prayer

I will seek after you, Lord for I know you are the truth. To hear others say that you are the truth is not enough, I want to know you personally, for myself. Your word declares that we shall know the truth, and it will set us free. I thank you for this promise.

A PROUD MAN

"You hurled me into the deep, into the very heart of the seas, and the currents swirled about me; all your waves and breakers swept over me." Jonah 2:3

Mighty Captain, man of pride,
Feared and honored far and wide,
But as a plant diseased by canker,
Naaman could not hide his rancor.

Maid and story, King and letter,
Seven dips to make a leper better,
Pride in prophets camp ignored,
A servant meets him at the door.

Rage awoke, like lion maimed,
Pride evoked, could now be tamed,
As pebbles smoothed by waves that toss,
To know I Am, you must be washed.

Dear Sister,

Have you ever felt God's cleansing waves? Naaman's pride hindered him from receiving his healing. God knows what keeps us from him, and because of his love he desires to rid us of all these obstacles and hindrances. His methods and his masterful ways are higher than ours. We cannot guess how he will free us or the means he will use to heal us. We can only, like lifeless stones and pebbles in a stream, accept the water sent to wash and smooth our rough surfaces. Yield to him, and you will find healing for the diseases of the heart. Let the Son make you every whit clean, as he has promised. Humble yourself in the sight of the Lord, and he will lift you up. The Master desires you to know him and the power of his marvelous molding. He is the Potter, and we are the clay. Look at all those who are marked by his touch. Is there not a beauty in them that you seek after in your deepest, most inward parts?

A Prayer

Lord, I will lay aside my pride, and be washed in the fountain that can purify. I will be cleansed by the fuller's soap. You are like a refiner's fire, and who am I to question your methods as you make me whole? I would be rid of all bitterness that has grown up to strangle my heart. Remove it with the waves of your powerful, cleansing love. Wash me, and I shall be clean. Purify me, and I shall be white as snow.

LION'S DEN

"Be self-controlled and alert. Your enemy the devil prowls around like a roaring lion looking for someone to devour. Resist him, standing firm in the faith, because you know that your brothers throughout the world are undergoing the same kind of sufferings." 1 Peter 5:8

A roar of fierce and violent sound
Rose up from den below the ground
The lions paced and roamed the rocks
The stone was moved, the man was brought,

And thrown among the hungry beasts
They rolled their tongues, they made to feast,
Their snarls rumbled low and mean,
More hostile faces never seen,

Until the angel shut their jaws
With mighty arm restrained their paws,
With awesome challenge, help appears,
To know I Am, you must not fear.

Dear Sister,

How terrifying to face the real lions Daniel spent the night with in the darkened den! How apprehensive we become when facing our enemy the lion in our own lives. The Word admonishes us not to flee when facing such battles, but to stand firm in the faith, knowing that behind us we have the support of God himself, who will enable us, restore us and make us strong. Along with this, we have the armor of God to gird ourselves. We are not unprotected, but required to use the weapons he has given us, the shield of faith, the sword of the Spirit, the name of Christ. If we only listen to the sounds of the roaring and snarling beasts, imagining our demise at their anxious paws, our sensibilities would indeed be overcome. Instead, we fortify our minds with the truth, the Word of God echoing in the deepest recesses of our hearts. We remember the promises he has given to us. We are his children, he loves us with a passion. Will he let us be overcome, while we trust him so completely in desperation? Won't he rescue us, shutting the mouths of the lions as he did for Daniel? He will, and speedily, for no one is able to snatch God's children from his hand. He has promised.

A Prayer

I must not give in to doubt. I believe you are willing to save me from the lions. Even in the most threatening situations, you have complete authority. I shall not fear, for you are always with me. I may trust in your complete and unfailing strength.

THE FURNACE

"For no one can lay any foundation other than the one already laid, which is Jesus Christ. If any man builds on this foundation using gold, silver, costly stones, wood, hay or straw, his work will be shown for what it is, because the Day will bring it to light. It will be revealed with fire, and the fire will test the quality of each man's work."
1 Corinthians 3:11-13

A golden idol towered high
The leaders, people, gathered nigh
At sound of flute, and harp and pipe
The crowd would bow and worship right.

O King, we will not offer praise
Three men insisted, fire blazed
With robes and turbans, men were bound,
And cast wherein the flames are found.

With Son of God, they walked unharmed
No fire scorched them, nothing burned
Like precious gold all men desire,
To know I Am, endure the fire.

Dear Sister,

How hot the fire that surrounded the three Hebrew
children, and how great their relief when they began to realize it
would not consume them! They took a stand, an outspoken
one, one that carried a price, and they prepared to suffer for it.
Is our testimony of Jesus as firmly planted in our hearts? Would
we, if necessary, have the strength and courage to face
punishment for our declaration that we will worship none but
the Great I Am? Let us build solidly on this foundation, the
foundation of Jesus Christ, and then the trial by fire will serve
to refine us instead of destroying us. Perhaps there will be that
first suspenseful moment, when we hold our breath and feel
the heat around us. Let us take courage in making our own
declaration for him, knowing that if the fire comes, he comes
also to share the place in the flames. Do not be afraid of the
fire, of refinement and purging, of testing and trial, for where
the fire is, his presence also dwells.

A Prayer

Lord, you are ever present, even in the darkest trials. Let me
trust in your promises. Let me make a stand to obey you even
when persecution will come as a result. Give me courage, and
let me stand where the flame shall not kindly upon me, for your
name's sake.

Linda McGinnis & Diane McGinnis

4
THE BATTLE

"For the battle is the Lord's…"
1 Samuel 17:47

AN UNPLEASANT TASK

"For our struggle is not against flesh and blood, but against the rulers, against the authorities, against the powers of this dark world and against the spiritual forces of evil in the heavenly realms. Therefore, put on the full armor of God, so that when the day of evil comes, you may be able to stand your ground, and after you have done everything, to stand."
Ephesians 6:12,13

Jael, woman wise and bold
As Deborah's song has often told
About the lady and the tent,
Inside which weary Sisera went.

Tired, thirsty, he did ask,
For water, and she opened flask
Of milk, and when he sipped the brew
With spike of tent she ran him through.

The enemy, by this destroyed,
Not man but woman filled the void,
Though battle sights are full of gore,
To know I Am, you fight the war.

Dear Sister,

Jael was strong in time of battle. She marked the enemy, and took drastic measures to defeat him. Israeli women were usually spared the unpleasantness of war. Perhaps Sisera knew this, and expected to take advantage of this vulnerable area of the Israelites camp. Jael was no weak link, in fact, she engineered his death. As Christian women, we too are in a spiritual war. How often the enemy spies out a woman, desiring to use her vulnerability to set up a stronghold. Satan tempted Eve in the garden. We must be on our guard! In readiness, wearing the full armor of God at all times, we will recognize the enemy when he appears. We must mark him, and fulfill the unpleasant task of defeating him with the sword of the Spirit. Do not doubt your resources, David prepared himself with only five smooth stones and a sling. It only took one of those stones to bring the mighty Goliath down. In the day of battle, call upon the name of the Lord. Make yourself strong in the power of his might. He makes victory swift and sure!

A Prayer

I will not war according to the flesh, but in the Spirit. Lord, be my Captain, and lead me into the fray. You are a God of valor and strength. Give me victory over the enemy of my soul. I will take up my shield and use the sword of God. Make my thrust accurate and deep. I will fight the battles you lead me to fight, and I won't go into battle unprepared or with a reckless heart.

ARMOR BEARER

"Jonathan said to his young armor bearer, 'Come, let's go over to the outpost of those uncircumcised fellows. Perhaps the Lord will act in our behalf. Nothing can hinder the Lord from saving, whether by many or by few.' 'Do all that you have in mind,' his armor bearer said. 'Go ahead; I am with you heart and soul.' "
1 Samuel.14:6,7

Heavy shield upon his arm
Son of King to keep from harm
Followed up the rocky crag
Optimistic, heart won't flag

Stop and wait, response to hear
Come and fight, lift up the spear
Climb, the Lord will help defeat
The Philistines, 'til they retreat

So right and left, the sword expelled,
An army fierce was soon repelled
As earthquake terrorizes throng
To know I Am, you must be strong.

Dear Sister,

We must pray for courage to face strong and formidable enemies with a valiant heart! And who is the Son we follow? A fierce, dread champion! We are not required to go into battle alone! The Son leads us into battle and directs our warfare, for we are in his service. His death has made us victorious. We have the easy part, entering into his victory. He has given us weapons, a shield for protection, and a sword to deal the enemy a potent blow. It is amazing that after these two brave men went out to face the enemy, God sent a panic among the soldiers that caused them to flee, and the ground shook with the sound of their retreat. God is able to deliver by many or by few, Jonathan said, and this is true today. Whether it be in the prayers of intercession, or physical words and acts which show our stand against the armies of darkness, we have the satisfaction of knowing beforehand the victory is ours, that it has been won for us by Christ. Will you be one of the few? Are you willing to climb up the rocky crags, following the Champion with a heart of courage? Take comfort! He leads us, and gives us weapons that are mighty for the pulling down of strongholds.

A Prayer

I will follow you, Lord, even into battle. I know that your strength is able to deliver, either by many, or by few. I will trust in your power and your might, even when faced with a mighty throng.

TASTE AND SEE

"The laws of the Lord are sure and altogether righteous. They are more precious than gold, than much pure gold; they are sweeter than honey, than honey from the comb."
Psalm 19:10

Battle weary, fading sound,
Honey oozed upon the ground
Tired army, hands were stayed
They feared the oath the King had made.

But one, unbound by oath or law
Dipped his staff and tasted raw,
The sweetness strengthened him anew
His eyes were brightened, heart was too.

A foolish curse upon the men
Who needed sustenance again
Like honey, wisdom feeds the soul,
To know I am, you must be full.

Dear Sister,

How many times do we come, weary and battle worn, into God's presence to be revived? Over, and over, to be sure. Jonathan revived himself with honey after the battle. We don't have to hesitate as we partake of the sustenance in the Word, the refreshing infilling of the Holy Spirit, the sweetness of resting in his presence. No one can stop us, or hold us back from the delightful blessings of communing with him. It is in his presence that our eyes are brightened with the sight of his beauty, and our hearts are encouraged by his overwhelming love. This is food for the soul, eating his words and digesting them in our inner man. Let no other man, no duty, no pleasure, keep you away from this necessary revival. Open your heart to the fountain of life, and let it flow within you as a river of living waters. Pursue the wisdom of God, seek after the truth, and let it work on your mind and heart. Your mind will be transformed, your soul will be renewed, and the times of refreshing will come upon you in fullness. There is no reason to be empty, or only half full, when God has made so much of himself available. Let your cup be full, let it overflow with the richness and sweetness that is found only in drawing near to Christ, in feeding upon his Word.

A Prayer

Lord, you have granted us blessings that are good and wonderful. Your word is rich in nourishment, and sweet to the taste. I thank you for supplying such special delights for my soul and spirit. You are a loving and gracious provider!

A WARRIOR'S CHARGE

*"Your servant has killed both the lion and the bear; this
uncircumcised Philistine will be like one of them, because he has
defied the armies of the living God."*
1 Samuel 17:36

Champion stood of giant strength
Nine feet tall with spear of length
Helmet bronze upon his head
Coat of mail, inspired dread

Challenged with a mocking shout
Choose your man and bring him out!
I defy your paltry ranks,
You will serve us and give thanks.

To the birds I'll give your flesh,
All the beasts will tear and thresh.
As raging storm is turned to peace,
To know I Am, you kill the beast.

Dear Sister,

Kill or be killed! What a terrible choice to face! David declared that death should come to Goliath, as payment for defying the armies of the living God. We have a choice, as well. Do we live in defeat, constantly beaten down by the oppressive threats of the enemy of our souls? Or do we put his lies to death, confronting each one with a stone of truth carried in our hearts? We are able to silence his intimidations and torments. David took no thought for his own size, his lack of stout weaponry, or his inexperience as a man of war. He knew that when he had faced other threats, such as a lion and a bear, he was able to conquer them with the weapon most familiar to him, the one closest to his hand. Let us store up the Word of God in our hearts. Small victories will lead to larger ones, and we will see that we can defeat the enemies taunts in our minds. We don't have to be slaves to a lie, we can kill the influence of the enemy in our lives by resisting him, and replacing his lies with the glorious words of truth.

A Prayer

Your word, Lord, is a powerful weapon. Let me always be ready to use it when I need to destroy the enemy. As David trained time and time again, and became skilled at using his sling, I must also train myself to use the Word of God accurately, and skillfully. Help me to stay in your Word!

DESPERATION

"Do you not say, 'Four months more and then the harvest'? I tell you, open your eyes and look at the fields! They are ripe for harvest... I sent you to reap what you have not worked for. Others have done the hard work, and you have reaped the benefits of their labor."
John 4:34,35,38

Lepers at the city gate
Speaking, in suspense they wait
Should we linger here to die?
About us famine, tell me why

Let us enter battle camp
Give surrender, take our chance
In agreement, four at dusk,
Footsteps sounded, hands were clutched

They wondered at the silent tents
Ate and drank, all defied sense
Like good news and a good report,
To know I Am, you must go forth.

Dear Sister,

If anyone ever reaped what they did not work for, it was the four lepers. Hungry and without resources, they took a risk that proved to have the makings of a miracle. The sound of their feet as they went forth into the enemy camp became as loud as the sound of a great army of horses and chariots, causing the Arameans to flee, leaving behind food, supplies, silver and gold in abundance. What would have happened if the four desperate men had remained at the gate, lamenting their situation, unwilling to take a step a faith? Sometimes the steps we take, though small, become infused with the awesome power of God even as we take them, and become precursors to mighty miracles for his name's sake. The steps of the four lepers brought food to the entire city, as they realized there was too much to keep to themselves. Bounty from heaven is available. We can state this with assurance, knowing the Lord has made provision for us in all things. There is no need for us to wait until we are sick with famine to enter into God's blessings. We can go forth now, today, and enter into the abundant life awaiting us. This is good news, and we can declare it with confidence as we go forth to do the will of the Father.

A Prayer

Lord, I need to take the step of faith when you have directed it, in order to receive the glorious bounty you have prepared for me. When I am in your will, my steps will be mighty and powerful indeed. Let me step boldly, freely, and enter into the blessings you have provided.

5
LOVE

"Love never fails…"
1 Corinthians 13:8

HARD LABOR

"Make it your ambition to lead a quiet life, to mind your own business and work with your hands, just as we told you, so that your daily life may win the respect of outsiders and so that you will not be dependent on anybody."
1 Thessalonians 4:11

Weak eyed Leah in the tent
Stood for sister, Jacob spent
Seven years in toil and work
Earned his wife, the payment took

Instead of one he loved so strong
The morning showed his choice was wrong
For in the night, behind the veil,
Weak eyes were hidden, told no tale

In silence, foiled, tricked, undone
Seven years work again begun
Like season oft, repeats each year,
To know I Am, you persevere.

Dear Sister,

Poor Jacob! Seven years is a long time to work for anything, but if the goal is worthy, the work must be done. How many times we learn and read of the patience required in the saints of old, who saw the promises, and had to wait patiently, sometimes knowing the fulfillment lay long in the future. We ourselves join Jesus when he says, my Father works, and I also work. Not works which earn us salvation, for that is free, but good works which reveal the power of God in our lives, works he assigns to us to bring God glory and honor. We work and toil, and sometimes it seems forever before we reap any sign of fruitful labor. May we depend upon God for the strength to do what he commands us. May we receive grace to persevere, in the face of long hours and no rewards. Jacob was willing to work so many years for the one he loved, without giving up. May we, also, work for the one we love, and may the time pass for us as if it were only a few days, because of our great love for the one we serve.

A Prayer

Father, as you know, I do not want to grow weary in well doing. You have promised we shall reap, if we faint not! Yet my flesh and my heart does fail. Lord, renew me and revive me! Give me fresh vision, and fresh love, that I may press on until the goal is reached.

A LOVE STORY

"I know that my redeemer lives, and that in the end he will stand upon the earth." Job 19:25

"Looking for that blessed hope, and the glorious appearing of the great God and our Savior, Jesus Christ; who gave himself for us, that he might redeem us from all iniquity, and purify unto himself a peculiar people, zealous of good works." Titus 2:13,14

Moabitess, dawn to dusk,
Working, gleaning, beating husk
Washed, anointed, and now dressed
To feet of Boaz while he rests

A load of barley in her veil
She left the floor, he would not fail
To buy her from a kinsman nearer,
For he loved and held her dearer.

Among the wheat he found her fair,
He loved, he bought, for he did care
As Ruth in field of wheat did glean,
To know I Am, you are redeemed.

Dear Sister,

How does God view that which is unwanted and left behind? As Ruth gathered in a field of wheat, God gathers men from the earth. Not many wise, not many mighty are called, but God has called the weak and the foolish to glorify himself. The nearer kinsman in Ruth's case did not want her, but there was one who not only wanted, but cherished her. So also, those who are rejected in this world can be joyful in their state, because there is one who loves them and will pay the price of their redemption. We cannot explain his great love for such as we are, poor, wretched, castaways! But rejoice, there is one who longs to bestow favor on us, and will gather us to himself with enthusiasm. There is one who will not rest until he accomplishes the deed this day. Surely, this is a beautiful love story. The price of our redemption was far greater than that of Ruth's. It involved Christ giving himself for us. For the greater sacrifice, greater love is required. In our case, it was the ultimate price. Christ showed us his incredible love, a love story above all others.

A Prayer

I will rejoice in my great redemption. Like Ruth, I am humbled by the love given to me in such a public and grand display. As Boaz hurried to redeem his love, so I thank you Lord for your swift response to my cry for mercy. I am full of joy, my redeemer lives!

THE RELEASE

"Who is like the Lord our God, the One who sits enthroned on high, who stoops down to look on the heavens and the earth? He settles the barren woman in her home as a happy mother of children. Praise the Lord."
Psalm 113:5,9

Sad and silent, drowned in despair,
She lipped a silent wordless prayer
Shaken in spirit, soul poured out,
Priest mistook for a drunken bout.

Son was given, her womb held child,
She loved him, suckled him a while,
Then weaned, and with a vow to pay,
She brought him up, to give away.

A coat, to cover tender skin,
Stitch by stitch, a prayer for him,
As rain to earth and back does flow,
To know I Am, you must let go.

Dear Sister,

A wise woman knows the Lord has given her a child for a season. Through God's grace, she will be able to give her child back to God. Hannah promised her son to God before he was conceived, and when he was born, she had only a few years to care for him before he was given to the priesthood. She cared for him tenderly, and then, at an early age, let him go. Her sacrifice, however, allowed for Samuel to become a great and powerful prophet. One thing we can be assured of as we release our children into the Lord's hands, he will be close to them. Samuel heard the audible voice of God at a young age, and God confirmed his purpose and calling. God also has a purpose and a plan for our children, and he will speak to them as well. It must have been a bittersweet parting for Hannah, as she took Samuel up to the Temple as promised. She could only see him once a year, but she never stopped loving him. She would bring him a coat when she came to visit, and what a beautiful labor of love that garment must have been. If we have children or loved ones, we will be required to let go of them in one way or another. Even so, we will never cease to love and pray for them. Whether you are able to see your child day in and day out, or only once a year, take the opportunity to cherish them. Give them their "coat", a symbol of your love.

A Prayer

Lord thank you for children and loved ones who fill my life. Help me to cherish them, and express my love for them in tangible ways. When the time comes, help me to release them into your hands, knowing you will be close to them and speak to their hearts. Help them to grow into your purpose and calling with strong and steady steps.

A WOMAN TO PRAISE

"Blessed are all who fear the Lord, who walk in
his ways." Psalm 128:1

"Charm is deceptive, and beauty is fleeting; but a woman who
fears the Lord is to be praised."
Proverbs 31:30

Morning early, she rises up,
To plan for day and fill his cup
And in the first of daytime light,
She prays and works with all her might.

Of flax, and wool and fabrics new,
She makes and sells more than a few
Her children and her husband say,
She is a blessing all the day.

In light and dark her candle's bright,
She's radiant, a stunning sight.
As fruitful vines yield blessed stores,
To know I Am, you fear the Lord.

Dear Sister,

The yoke of the Lord is easy, and his burden is light. Fearing the Lord is certain to produce fruit in the life of a believer. This fruit forms and ripens by a natural process. It is not a laborious task to become a woman who is to be praised, like the Proverbs 31 woman. Some women believe it is almost unobtainable. As easily and naturally as a well cared for grape vine yields bountiful stores, we as women can yield the fruit of the spirit as we are cared for by the master husbandman. The one who cares for us is the Lord himself. This fruit causes us to be of great value in the eyes of our husbands and children. It is a source of blessing and contentment to those around us. A woman who is praised is one who gives her talent, ambitions, and even her mundane tasks to God, praying that they will bring him glory. She is not afraid to contradict the current definition of womanhood, her fear of God gives her courage to be different. Her heart, filled with love, is not idle, but filled to overflowing with the desire to bless her family. Fearing God is the source of her beauty, joy, strength, and love. The woman described beautifully by Solomon can be a reality. You can be such a woman. With God, it is possible!

A Prayer

Lord, I desire to be a woman who fears you above all else. I would have you tend my heart, so that I may yield the blessed stores of peace and contentment to my family. Help me as I love those you have given me, serving them with my hands, seeing to their needs. May I grow in grace as I pour out my life. May my home be a haven and a refuge for all who dwell there.

A WAY HOME

"It is of the Lord's mercies we are not consumed, because his compassions fail not. They are new every morning: great is thy faithfulness."
Lamentations 3:22,23

Fifteen pieces, a homer and a half
Bought a wife with an adulterous past
Hosea sought for her, high and low
Where did she flee? Why did she go?

He found her on a platform of shame
Men were bidding, making their claim,
But he rose to the fore, love for his bride,
Extending his hand like the rush of a tide

He reached out to hold her and carry away,
The one he loved, for his love would not sway
Like ocean tide faithful, washes the shore,
To know the I Am, you must be restored.

Dear Sister,

As the earth and shore stand eternally connected, so too are we forever joined to our eternal Lord. We might ask, "where shall I go from your spirit?" Where could we ever hide from his all pervading presence? It is impossible. For we would conclude, "if I go to heaven, You are there, if I go to the depths of hell, You are there. And if I take the wings of the morning and dwell in the uttermost parts of the sea; even there shall your hand lead me, and your right hand shall hold me." Rejoice, for this is true. Our Lord has betrothed us to himself. He has promised himself to us, and set his seal upon us. Nothing can separate us from his love. He loves us so much that even when we fall, he restores us to himself. He restores us with his great forgiveness, his wonderful presence and his manifold blessings. They will flow back to us, just as the ocean tide returns again in its ebb and flow. We can praise him for his marvelous loving kindness. We bless him with thankful hearts, for though we fail, his compassions fail not.

A Prayer

Lord, grateful I am for your mercies, which are new each morning, and your compassions which never fail. Even when I have fallen, you search me out with your forgiving heart, and restore me to yourself. Thank you for the faithful tide of your love which continues to wash over me days without number I will reach out my arms, and return your love with my whole being.

Linda McGinnis & Diane McGinnis

6
DECEPTIONS, FAILURES, SAD EVENTS

"Do not be deceived…"
Galatians 6:7

SUBSTANCE OF LIFE

"Woe to him who quarrels with his Maker, to him who is but a potsherd among the potsherds on the ground. Does the clay say to the potter, What are you making?" Isaiah 45:9
"Yet, O Lord, you are our Father. We are the clay, you are the potter; we are all the work of your hand."
Isaiah 64:8

Dust lay on the ground sleeping
Formless, void, no shape keeping
Settled, without life and destiny,
An earthen clay that needed heaven's key

Then Master's touch swirled upon the ground
The finger wrote without a sound
And he emerged, a masterpiece of life,
Lacked one thing only, friend and wife.

So sleeping still, his rib became,
Further beauty, with a name
Clouds turn from dust to whirling storm,
To know I Am, you must be formed.

Dear Sister,

What patience and fortitude is required while we sit upon the Potter's wheel! We did not make ourselves, shaping our form, our personality, our gifts. Just as God made Adam, he takes charge of our formation, and we behold a vessel made from clay, formed for a noble purpose. Without the outpouring of his love and mercy, we are a frail and breakable vessel. When he fills us with his life, then the vessel may serve a heavenly commission. Let us not forget it is his hand at work, and not our own. We must allow this formation, as he shapes us and makes us into the vessel he destined us to be. His plan for us, written in his book before there was time, is one to which we are perfectly fitted and created. Do you see a flaw in yourself? Did the hand of the Potter shake? He shapes the clay as he sees fit. Blessed is the man who waits, and yields the reins of his life into the one who sees all, and knows all. The Master Potter doesn't make mistakes, and sets the pot among his vessels to be used for glory. Let him form you. Watch and marvel at his skill, his artistry, his experience. You will be amazed at the vessel you become, when you fully yield to Him.

A Prayer

I will yield completely to the Master Potter. In your hands, I become a vessel of honor, and a perfectly formed piece of handiwork. This is my desire, to be shaped and molded by you, and changed into your image. On your wheel, I shall offer my dust, and dirt and clay. I will let you form me, Lord and Father, into something of value and purpose!

A CRAFTY LURE

"But I am afraid that just as Eve was deceived by the serpents cunning, your minds may somehow be led astray from your sincere and pure devotion to Christ." 2 Corinthians 11:3
"No temptation has seized you except what is common to man. And God is faithful; he will not let you be tempted beyond what you can bear. But when you are tempted, he will also provide a way out so that you can stand up under it."
1 Corinthians 10:13

Woman in the paradise alone,
Temptation came to her in crafty tone
For from all trees to freely eat,
Forbidden pleasure did compete.

The hiss of cunning serpent did convey
An error and the urge, forsake the way
Dark words that lured and still revealed,
The futile goal, "like God" appealed.

Then good for food, and eye, and being wise
The sole command of God she did despise,
Like ship cast on the waves to list,
To know I Am, you must resist.

Dear Sister,

Resist the devil, and he will flee from you. Eve did not. This seems a simple admonition to follow, until the actual temptation surrounds us with its lures and promises of pleasure or fulfillment. Too bad the pleasure promised always turns out to be a lie. How often have we given in, and been left desolate in choices of our own making? There is no reward for disobedience, only sorrow and regrets. How wary we must be, having the Word of God hidden in our hearts, that we might not sin against him. How sure we should be of his commands, having them clear and unmistakable in our minds, and therefore not susceptible to accepting a half truth or a twisted one. He bought forgiveness for us, and we receive it, but how often only after paying a price of our own in reaping the folly we have fallen into. And yet Paul writes, a way of escape is at hand! May God give us eyes to see the way of our escape in the midst of our temptation. May he give us the strength to resist, to count forbidden pleasure worth denying for his sake. May he help us flee sin and its repercussions, and fear the Great I Am more than we desire to indulge our lusts and selfishness. Let us find comfort in knowing his grace is sufficient. He will reveal to us the way of escape, only let us be committed to taking it.

A Prayer

Father, temptations and crafty lures appeal strongly to my flesh. I am weak, and I shall surely fall if I walk in the flesh. My prayer is that my spirit, alive unto you, will be strong and committed to escaping the pitfalls and snares laid for me. Fill me with your spirit, that I might not fulfill the desires of the flesh.

A SAD DAY

"Then the man and his wife heard the sound of the Lord God as he was walking in the garden in the cool of the day, and they hid from the Lord God among the trees of the garden. But the Lord God called to the man, Where are you?" Genesis 3:8,9

"I was found by those who did not seek me; I revealed myself to those who did not ask for me."
Romans 10:20

In the garden many trees
Rivers, gold, and food to please
Without clothes and without shame,
To man and woman, sorrow came.

And in the cool of ending day
The Father's presence, voice did say,
Calling out with tender care
Where, O Adam, are you, where?

Amid the paradise He made,
The two stood huddled, sad, afraid,
For like the raindrops sun has dried,
To know I Am, you must not hide.

Dear Sister,

How grateful we are that God did not leave Adam in his sad and sorrowful state, but came to the garden looking for him. He didn't let the sin in the garden separate himself from the man he made and loved. He came to Adam and Eve, clothing them in garments of his own making. How quickly he clothes us also, with the garments of righteousness purchased for us by Christ's death. He who knew no sin, bore our sin upon his own body, so that we might be made right with our Creator. He made a way to forgive Adam and Eve, for from the beginning his plan of salvation was in place, the lamb was slain from the foundations of the world. And yet we hide from his all seeing eye! We cower in shame and sorrow, when he has made a way to extend mercy and forgiveness to us. Step out into the light, and let your tears of sorrow be dried in the sunshine of his love. We have no reason to hide from a God who provided salvation by his own hand, with the sacrifice of his only Son. How he loves us and searches us out! How our hearts fill with repentance at the sign of his mercy. Do not hide, but come boldly to the throne of grace to receive mercy in your time of need. Let nothing stop you from entering his presence. He will dry your tears, and replace them with joy.

A Prayer

Why should I hide, when I hear your voice calling so lovingly for me? You know all about my painful mistakes, and yet you still seek me out. I will show myself, for at your feet I can receive forgiveness. As I look toward you, I will experience the sunshine of your love.

THE BLOOD CRIES

*"If anyone says, I love God, yet hates his brother, he is a liar.
For anyone who does not love his brother, whom he has seen,
cannot love God, whom he has not seen. And he has given us
this command: Whoever loves God must also love his brother."*
1 John 4:20,21

Brothers two, of Adam's seed
Brought offering, a noble deed,
One the fruits of farming life,
One a firstborn sacrifice

Favor granted from the throne
Praised the gift of one alone
Cain was angry, face aflame,
Heart embittered, rage would reign,

Took the blood of guiltless man
In the field, no witness planned
But eyes of heaven never sleep,
To know I Am, your brother keep.

Dear Sister,

The eyes of heaven are watching over us, seeing all we do. They roam to and fro across the earth, strengthening those whose hearts are committed to him. How then should we live? We should love our brother. This takes time and effort, resources, and giving from the heart. Sometimes our own families are the hardest to love, because they are our flesh and blood, a fixed part of our life. Where is our brother this very minute? Does he need a friend, someone to share the love of God with him, someone to give it unconditionally, as it was given to us? Cain was full of jealousy and resented the righteous act his brother did. We should banish jealousy and resentment from our hearts, they only grow into bitter roots that lodge within to plague us and poison all we do. Before Cain took his brother out to the field, God spoke to him, encouraging him to deal with the problem that was so evident by his downcast countenance. If sin is crouching at our door, we should follow the advice given to Cain, master it! This love we are to have for our brother: a love without envy, a love that appreciates the gifts and qualities he has received. This shows the depth of our love for the heavenly Father. Since it reveals so much, should we not strive to open our hearts to the brothers and sisters surrounding us, to love them, as he has first loved us? Let the love of God be shed abroad in our hearts!

A Prayer

What glorious love is found in you, Lord, so sincere, so pure, and without envy! Could I love my brother like this? It seems so far beyond my reach, but I know you can provide me with this love. Let it flow from the high and heavenly throne above down into every deep and hidden recess of my heart. .

JUST A GLANCE

"And Jesus said unto him, No man, having put his hand to the plough, and looking back, is fit for the kingdom of God."
Luke 9:62

"Do not say, 'Why were the old days better than these?' For it is not wise to ask such questions."
Ecclesiastes 7:10

Escape for life, the angel's plea
And do not look behind thee!
Linger not, but make great haste,
The cities and the plains will waste!

The warning rang in their dull ears,
Sons-in law just mocked and jeered
Angels seized the daughter's hands
From destruction they all ran

Lot had a disobeying mate
A salty stack became her fate
As butterfly leaves cocoon sack,
To know I Am, you don't look back.

Dear Sister,

A moth or butterfly races away from his old cocoon, setting his sights on the new world he has entered. We too, must race forth to what we have been prepared for, and we should not look back. When Lot left Sodom and Gomorrah, he was warned not to look back. How has the Lord ordered your steps? Have you set your sights on the path he has marked for you? How shall you safely step from destruction and bondage unless you are looking in the right direction? What lies behind is death, destruction, and things that are old. Ahead is something God has prepared in his mercy. We make a choice about what we will focus on. The choice we make reveals a lot about what we value most. When God is leading us from one place to another, we must trust that he knows best. He has prepared our way, so we can pursue our goal swiftly and whole heartedly. We must value his will above all else. When we choose to honor God by having our eyes turned in his direction, none of our steps will slide. He will lead us into newness of life, and from glory to glory.

A Prayer

Lord, lead me on, I will follow when you show me the way. Help me to leave behind the old things in my life, the sin that so easily besets me, the worries of yesterday. When you order my steps, I know I will not stumble. I will turn my eyes to behold you, and hear a voice behind me saying, "This is the way, walk ye in it." By your grace I will go forward, and with your help, I will not look back.

A JEALOUS PLOT

"You shall not covet your neighbor's house. You shall not covet your neighbor's wife, or his manservant or maidservant, his ox or donkey, or anything that belongs to your neighbor."
Exodus 20:17

Grazing flocks, one sought his kin
Yet from afar, they shaped a whim
From Father he received a coat,
So ornamented, he does gloat,

He dreamed of sun, and moon, and stars,
His sheaf of grain ruled over ours,
Let us kill the dreaming boy,
A plot and scheme they did employ

A brother's plea, so shortly heard
They stripped his robe, for envy lured
Like grave unyielding, fire hot,
To know I Am, you covet not.

Dear Sister,

How tempting it is sometimes to compare our lives with those around us. Joseph's brothers acted out of envy of him, and resented how their father loved him. We see others and their material blessings, and wish for more. Or we look with envy at their gifts and accomplishments, talents and even facets of their appearance, wishing to change things about ourselves. This habit will only lead us down a road of discontentment and frustration. Before long we become blind to the manifold blessings God has poured into our own lives, into our own families. Have we health? It is a priceless gift. We can be grateful to God! Have we food and clothing? Let us be content. God has provided for our needs. Even beyond these physical necessities, he has given us gold, refined in the fire, which cannot be bought, white clothes to wear, and salve for our blind eyes, that we might see. For all these heavenly gifts, have we given thanks? Let us not neglect to show him our gratitude, by being satisfied and content with the place we are in as we seek to follow him. Let us also give thanks for the multitude of gifts he has placed in others, members of his body, and never desire to trade material wealth for the peace and joy that comes from a close fellowship with God. We have so much, let us turn away our eyes from sights of what we have not, and open our eyes to all he has given us.

A Prayer

Lord, I thank you for the abundant life you have given me. I will be content, if I walk close to you. No matter the struggles I face, there are blessings all around me.

A CHANGED PLAN

*"And we urge you, brothers, warn those who are idle, encourage
the timid, help the weak, be patient with everyone."*
1 Thessalonians 5:14

*"Defend the cause of the weak and fatherless; maintain the
rights of the poor and oppressed. Rescue the weak and needy;
deliver them from the hand of the wicked."*
Psalm 82:3,4

Brother pleaded brother's cause,
Shed no blood, and break no laws
To hurt him I cannot allow
So throw him in the cistern now

Then went out, neglected noon,
Thinking, I will rescue soon,
Instead the brother's plan assailed,
A merchant's caravan prevailed

And Reuben to the place returned
Found no brother, stomach churned,
As skin a covering with effect,
To know I Am, you must protect.

Dear Sister,

A charge is given to us to help our weaker brothers, to defend them, to stand in the gap, to plead their cause! Reuben failed to protect his younger brother, he missed his opportunity to rescue. What godly behavior we exhibit when we rescue those whose voice is too weak or small to stand firm on their own. For isn't our God a dread champion to us? A warrior who rides on a white horse, leading many to victory? What censure is brought to the leaders in God's kingdom who have neglected to strengthen the weak, or bind up the injured. Jesus, standing in the Temple at the beginning of his ministry, declared he had been sent to proclaim freedom for the prisoners and release for the oppressed, as he proclaimed the year of the Lord. Is your brother downtrodden, misused, abused? Will you intercede for him, bringing down the mercies of God upon his head? Let us remember the widows, the orphans, the unloved, the despairing, and the hurting people of this world. We have the balm of Gilead, it must be applied. As he has protected us, and strengthened us, let us do the same for the ones who are in need, the ones too weak to speak. Let us defend them with conviction.

A Prayer

I can no longer close my eyes to the evil that seeks my brother's hurt. To stand idly by, and hope for a better time, will yield despairing results. Father, give me the power to free and save my brother in this present hour. Let me go in your strength, to free the prisoners, to loose those in bondage. Let me act swiftly, and not miss the opportunities before me now.

A YOUNG MAN

"Then she called to him, 'Samson - the Philistines are upon you!'" He awoke from his sleep and thought, "I'll go out as before and shake myself free." But he did not know that the Lord had left him. Then the Philistines seized him, gouged out his eyes and took him down to Gaza. Binding him with bronze shackles, they set him to grinding in the prison. But the hair on his head began to grow again after it had been shaved."
Judges 16:20-22

Strong, undaunted and unwise
A youth of iron will and lusting eyes
He broke a vow, his hair was sheared
His weakness like the morning dew appeared.

A crowd is there, a scorning laugh
A sound of mockery to wound and crack
A proud spirit, a challenge faced alone
With pain he stretches arms with aching bones.

Like rose that gives its finest scent at night
A humbling in obscurity restores the fight
As trees bow to the wind in yonder field
To know I Am, a man must yield.

Dear Sister,

There is a time in life when we feel strong, like Samson, having confidence in our ability to free ourselves from the many obstacles which might entrap us. We'd be the first to claim we are trusting in God's strength, but inside, we are banking on our ability to go out as before, relying on our knowledge, experience, or even gifts God has graciously given us. How necessary it is, how crucial, to remain dependant on God's strength no matter what the situation. There are times the Lord allows us to fall, times when we make wrong choices, overestimate our abilities, or think we can handle something that is out of our league. He is merciful, yes, but a righteous man falls seven times, and rises up again. We learn from times like these, and like Samson, our hair begins to grow again. It is the hand of the Lord that strips us of our reliance on human strength and wisdom. Undealt with, our self-strength will lead us to disaster. Let us yield, and bow in acknowledgment, it is his strength alone that carries us through our lives. We should remain humble servants, as those who humble themselves in the sight of the Lord will be lifted up. Those who fall are not forgotten, but are given the opportunity to cast aside the garments of pride and replace them with the cloak of humility.

A Prayer

Lord, the only sure confidence is in you. May I give you the glory for my victories, and acknowledge all might and power belong to you. May I lay aside the cloak of pride, and wear about my shoulders a mantle of humility.

SECRET SIN

"If we confess our sins, he is faithful and just to forgive us our sins, and to cleanse us from all unrighteousness." 1 John 1:9

"The sacrifices of God are a broken spirit: a broken and contrite heart, O God, thou wilt not despise."
Psalm 51:7

Bathing beauty, on the roof
Naked, lovely, fair in truth
He spied her washing, heart was slain
His eye unholy; mind profaned

His bed, in lust at once defiled
With cunning craft a scheme was wiled,
Her husband killed in battle's plight
But Nathan came to bring the light.

The sin in secret was revealed
A rich man from a poor did steal,
Like burdens on a beast do press,
To know I Am, you must confess.

Dear Sister,

When we commit a sin, as David did, we may find ourselves in denial. Afraid to admit and face what we have done, we find a way to sweep it under the carpet. We soon discover that our guilt does not go away. God chastens those he loves, and so the Lord finds a way to prick our conscience. In David's case, it was Nathan the prophet who was sent to speak about David's sin in a symbolic story. With his hidden sin exposed by Nathan, David sought for God's mercy in a heartfelt confession. We read his words of repentance in Psalm 51. Isn't it comforting to know there is one who is able to remove our sin far from us, as far as the east is from the west? We can confess all of our sins into Christ's holy ear, and we are promised forgiveness when we do so. David's confession is written and preserved in the Psalms, where his tender words were sent heavenward with weeping and pleading. It may break your heart to confess your sin, but a broken and contrite heart the Lord will not despise. He will grant you mercy, if only you confess.

A Prayer

Lord, I repent in dust and ashes. My sin weighs upon me, and presses me down. I confess my lack of faith, my selfishness, my pride. My heart is sorry, and I ask you to forgive all my transgressions. You alone have the power to remove my sin, casting it into the sea, never to be seen again. Wash me, and I shall be clean. Cleanse me, and I shall be white as snow. Remove the guilt, and I shall know true peace within my soul.

A TRAGEDY

"Do not take revenge, my friends, but leave room for God's wrath, for it is written: It is mine to avenge; I will repay, says the Lord." Romans 12: 19

"The Lord is slow to anger, and great in power; he will not leave the guilty unpunished."
Nahum 1:2

Comely daughter of the King
Drawn to chamber, ministering,
Kneaded dough, and shaped the bread,
Baked, and served by Amnon's bed.

Once alone his purpose clear
Of God's law he had no fear
She would yield, for marriage wait
He despised, did violate

Now hate for her, so undeserved,
He sent her out, she felt a scourge,
Like pain compounded, our revenge,
To know I Am, let God avenge.

Dear Sister,

Like the prophets of old, we inquire of God, 'why does the way of the wicked prosper?' Tamar struggled when Amnon abused her and cast her aside. Why is justice long in coming to those who have hurt others, those who destroy lives without compunction? One of the hardest things in life is to forgive when we have been wronged, not only wronged, but injured, crushed, and devastated. It is in these situations that we want to cry out to God to bring his righteous judgment, to punish those who have so callously wounded us. We must rest assured that not only will justice come in the end, but there is a Day of Judgment set aside, a day of reckoning for the deeds of men. This judgment must be left in the hands of one who has the power to judge rightly. For us, we are urged to display mercy and compassion, forgiving the debts of those who hurt us, knowing we ourselves have been forgiven of all. Perhaps the one who hurt you will find the mercy and forgiveness of God, perhaps he will repent of his wicked ways. Even if he doesn't, we must leave the outcome to the one who sits on the Great White Throne. There are times when we suffer on the earth. Jesus has stored up our tears in his bottle, taken note of our sorrows, and written them in his books. He will not forget.

A Prayer

Lord, you know all my deep and secret hurts. With your help, I must forgive and lay aside my desire to avenge. Lord, give me grace, I pray.

Linda McGinnis & Diane McGinnis

7
THE PROPHETS

"God will send you a prophet…"
Acts 7:37

TWO DREAMS

"Remember those in prison as if you were their fellow prisoners,
and those who are mistreated as if you yourselves were suffering."
Hebrews 13:3

"May the groans of the prisoners come before you;
by the strength of your arm preserve those condemned to die."
Psalm 79:11

Birthday celebration nigh
Feast prepared, officials high
Toasted Pharaoh, praised his rule
Returned cupbearer to his stool

He squeezed the grapes into the cup
He held it there while Pharaoh supped
The baker, though, as Joseph told,
Was hanged upon a grim scaffold

The news was brought, the dreams were true,
The danger passed for him who knew,
But one remained in prison shut,
To know I Am, do not forget.

Dear Sister,

Joseph was left forgotten in prison for a season. What sad fate awaits the prisoners who have never heard of the love of God, of his great salvation, of his abundant life! And we, such a short time ago, shared their fate, ourselves walking in darkness and ignorance of the glorious gospel of Christ. Remember the prisoners, we are told. There are those among us, who walk in our midst with the chains of the prison cell hanging about their forms. We have the key, the means to their freedom, the knowledge of the Savior. Should we not share it freely, disregarding the dank and dark surroundings while we bring a soul into the light of the truth? "When I was in prison," Jesus said, "you visited me." We should do this for the least of our brethren, remembering that there are others who long to join us in the feast. We should not get so caught up in the delights of God that we forget those who can so easily be released to join us. Let us mention their names to the King, pleading on their behalf for mercy and forgiveness, which the King is authorized to give. In all of our abundant life, let us remember that there are others who need remission of their sins, release from the prisons, and the news of the great salvation of God.

A Prayer

Lord, you have been such an example of compassion and love. I remember those who are shut away, and ask you to minister to them. I pray that they too, might be able to praise you for your salvation. They need you, Lord. Save, deliver, wash and heal them.

A DEEPER LOOK

"But the Lord said to Samuel, 'Do not consider his appearance or his height, for I have rejected him. The Lord does not look at the things man looks at. Man looks at the outward appearance, but the Lord looks at the heart.' "
1 Samuel 16:7

Saul's rejected, why now grieve?
Fill your horn with oil, leave
Seek out Jesse and his sons
From their tribe I've chosen one.

Surely him, he stands so fine,
Eldest, choicest, most divine.
Do not look upon his height
Or his outward features bright

Deeper does the Master delve
Into the heart, a man's own well
Like virgin is a cherished bride
To know I Am, you look inside.

Dear Sister,

Oh, the beauty and importance of a man finding his bride a virgin on the wedding night! And yet this condition is one unseen by the outward eye. It is a condition of purity, of being saved for the special person in your life whom you will marry. All the exterior qualities we exhibit can disguise the true condition in our heart, but we can't disguise ourselves before the Lord. He sees beneath the surface, beyond the platitudes we utter, past the defenses we raise to keep others at arm's length. It is a comfort to know there is one who sees us in all our failings and shortcomings, and still loves us unconditionally. He asks us, also, not to judge by what we see with our eyes. We are to listen for his assessment of each situation, which helps us in the decisions we make. Do you need a friend? You might pick one, based on qualities you see, and even these visible attributes sometimes accurately reflect the state of the person's inner life. But God sees more. He knows which friend will be right for you, which person will fit best with the carrying out of his will in your life. We can trust his judgment. Ours often fails. How we need insight for living! Let us ask for wisdom to see beyond the surface issues confronting us. Let us look deeper than human eyes can fathom. Let us see things as they truly are, let us see as he does.

A Prayer

You, Lord, in your ultimate wisdom, can show me the way to judge a righteous judgment, not based on the outward signs, but on what is found inside. I need your guidance as I choose the friends who will be a part of my life. Let me be open to love the ones you place on my heart even now.

WAILING WIND AND WHISPER

*"The Lord said, 'Go out and stand on the mountain
in the presence of the Lord, for the Lord is about to pass by.' "
1 Kings 19:11*

*"And these are but the outer fringe of his works; how faint
the whisper we hear of him! Who then can understand the
thunder of his power?"
Job 26:14*

Go and stand on mountain's cleft
Oh, you now fearful, faith bereft,
For I will soon pass by this place,
Though none has ever seen my face

Then mighty wind so turbulent
Tore at the stone, and mountain bent
An earthquake shook and jarred the rock
Then fire burned and seared the spot

And last a gentle whisper rose,
And drew man in a tranquil pose
Like voice that breaks and splits the wall
To know I Am, you must hear all.

Dear Sister,

How terrifying for Elijah to hear the sounds of fierce winds, the shaking of the earth, the burning of the elements! How comforting to have this loudness followed by the gentle voice of the Master. He would break down the walls and hard places in our hearts so his voice can find entrance and be heard. And yet, like Job, we wonder how the God of awesome power and glory can make himself so quiet, so tender, so still and small in our ears. How restful to have your ear attuned to his peaceful voice. It is a contrast indeed to the thundering sounds around us. We must learn to shut out the noise of the world, but at the same time we allow him to speak what he desires into our lives, whether it be loud or soft. We must wait in the secret place, in the cleft of the rock, anticipating his coming and our fellowship with him. We must see what he reveals to us about himself, not dictating to him what we would like to know, but accepting what he shows to us. Stand in the mountain's hiding place, and listen well. Shrink not from the unexpected sounds, but wait for the inevitable consolation, the whisper of the loving, still, small voice. He will call you by your name.

A Prayer

Lord, how wonderful to hear your still small voice. I will hide in the rock, and wait for you to come and speak. Your sheep hear your voice, and I will know when it is you who speaks.

A CHOICE

"Do not withhold good from those who deserve it, when it is in your power to do it." Proverbs 3:27

"Anyone, then, who knows the good he ought to do and doesn't do it, sins." James 4:17

A mantle from the prophet falls to earth,
A chariot departs with flaming girth
Stunned, yet seeing this display
A double portion rests on him today.

Then a town, a brackish well
A new bowl and the salt into it fell,
Some youths to jeer a balding man
Used to heal the water and the failing land.

With hasty words and uttered quick
The power of our God can wound and prick
Like thorns upon the stem abide,
To know I Am, you must decide.

Dear Sister,

When Elisha was blessed with Elijah's anointing, he had a choice to make. What responsibility we have when we bear the name of Christ upon our hearts! What opportunity to do good to others, to intercede for them, to encourage them. And yet with this ability to bring good and the good news into the lives of others, comes the danger of misusing the powerful word and name of God. If we err in our teaching, or hold to false ideas about God, we might influence others in the wrong direction. We could pressure them according to our own agenda instead of directing them into the will of God. If so, we will face a heavy accountability in the day of reckoning. Does he not tell us that to lead a little one astray is worse than death? How careful we should be as we bear the strength that lies in the powerful Word of God, exacting and watchful of our motives and actions. We should always hold up our hearts before the throne of Almighty God. At the same time, we should not fear as we follow the directives he gives us in bringing the light of the glory of the gospel of Jesus Christ to all who need him. In this pursuit, for his glory and honor, we have access to the great storehouse of his gifts and power to deliver. May we use the gifts of God with wisdom and care, to help the lost and hurting we come upon in this journey of life.

A Prayer

Lord, I need you to teach me the best way to share the gospel to those around me. Let me use the power and authority of Christ to bind up the broken-hearted, and aid the hurting.

A MESSENGER

"The preparations of the heart in man, and the answer of the tongue, is from the Lord." Proverbs 16:1

"Create in me a clean heart, O God; and renew a right spirit within me. Cast me not away from thy presence; and take not thy holy spirit from me. Restore unto me the joy of thy salvation; and uphold me with thy free spirit. Then will I teach transgressors thy ways; and sinners shall be converted unto thee."
Psalm 51:10-13

He saw, the year Uzziah died,
A throne and seraphim that cried,
A Holy Lord, his glory great,
He also saw his wretched state,

Unclean, undone, and filled with shame
An angel brought a coal aflame.
Touched his lips, he then was cleansed,
Who shall go? Who can I send?

As fire touched gold can thus be bent,
Messenger touched can now be sent
Like echo off deep canyon wall,
To know I Am, you answer the call.

Dear Sister,

If we meet with God, like Isaiah did, and receive the cleansing coal upon our lips, we can then answer God's call to our lives. When we behold God's glory, kneeling in worship as he reveals himself, we are in a position to be purified for service. If we are commissioned by the Lord, we can go where he sends us with confidence. Only God can prepare you for missionary service, whether home or abroad. You must wait for him to reveal his perfect will and purpose for your life, and then yield as he directs you to a specific place. Isaiah was willing, available, and quick to answer God's call. God made the necessary preparations and empowered his servant. When we receive a heavenly vision and undergo purification, then we will be effective ministers. Do we have a desire to glimpse his holiness? Do we desire to be purified and sent? Will we wait for him? He will give us a call, a commission, and the confidence to accomplish his work. Like Isaiah, let us declare, "Here am I, Lord, send me."

A Prayer

Lord, I am unclean, as Isaiah was. Let the coal from your holy fire cleanse not only my lips, but my heart. A vision of your beauty leaves me speechless with awe. I would go where you would send. Speak the word, Lord, and by your grace I will serve you forever.

A PAINFUL PRICE

"…yet now I am happy, not because you were made sorry, but because your sorrow led you to repentance."
2 Corinthians 7:9

Jonah in the belly pale
With sickening smell, appointed whale,
The seaweed twined about his head
In agony, a painful bed

As hours passed in darkness vile
Cried out with blind despair awhile
Until the mercy came once more,
And whale did spew him on the shore

So shaken, bleached and changed inside,
He set out preaching city wide
The courage from above will come,
To know I Am, you must not run.

Dear Sister,

Has there ever been a time in your life when, knowing what God required of you, you packed up, as it were, and ran in the opposite direction? Or maybe, in a moment of recklessness, you committed an act you knew was against God's will for your life? Or perhaps, when given instructions from the throne, you tarried, procrastinating or postponing the fulfilling of a divine commission? How like Jonah we are, when we find ourselves in the dregs which are the direct result of our disobedience! It is a terrible thing to suffer consequences, when we are well aware they were brought on by choices and decisions we made ourselves. This is especially true when we were in perfect awareness of how we were about to err, and acted rashly anyway. How we wish to undo our reckless sins! How thankful and grateful we are to the Lord, when he forgives our sin and restores his wonderful presence and peace to our lives. May God help us as we strive to walk in obedience, by granting us a willing spirit and a heart ready to do his will. Forget not the lessons learned in the belly of the whale, and may those mistakes never be repeated!

A Prayer

Lord, thank you for your ever loving heart that bends toward me in forgiveness. Help me not to run from your revealed will in my life.

Linda McGinnis & Diane McGinnis

8
HERALDS

"Prepare the way for him…"
Luke 1:76

A QUIET HEART

"You did not choose me, but I chose you to go and bear fruit—fruit that will last." John 15:16

"But we ought always to thank God for you, brothers loved by the Lord, because from the beginning God chose you to be saved through the sanctifying work of the Spirit and through belief in the truth." 2 Thessalonians 2:13

Prophecy from angel telling
Maiden in a humble dwelling
Highly favored, chosen womb,
Visitation soon would loom,

How will this be to one so pure?
In God alone is power sure
Son that shall be born so great
His throne an everlasting state.

May it be as you declare!
The messenger departs from there.
As flowers by a hand are picked,
To know I Am, he will select.

Dear Sister,

What joy is ours when we discover we have been chosen by the hand of God! What honor and privilege is ours to be selected as the recipient of God's grace and favor. Mary, singled out by angelic messenger, incredulous, but possessing a heart that yielded itself up to God, is our example. According to the words of the angel, the Holy Spirit was going to come upon her, and the power of the Most High would overshadow her. The honor of physically bearing the Christ child was hers. For us, we can carry the beauty of the Christ child within our hearts. We have the great honor of bearing fruit and giving out tidings of the heavenly news to all. It is good for us to remember that unless he had sought us out and loved us first, we would still be in darkness. He tells us that many are called, and indeed we share in giving out his call to the lost, but few are chosen. He has chosen us! Let us give thanks for the sovereign hand of God upon our lives, humbly recognizing the love that was bestowed on us at the moment of our salvation.

A Prayer

Your providence reigns supreme! I cannot explain your ways or your times. I simply rejoice that you select according to your perfect wisdom. Oh, the grace that is bestowed! I cannot speak, except to thank you humbly with a quiet heart for saving me.

VOICE OF LIFE

*"Through Jesus, therefore, let us continually offer to God a
sacrifice of praise-- the fruit of lips that confess his name."
Hebrews 13:15*

*"Declare his glory among the nations, his marvelous deeds
among all peoples." Psalm 96:3*

Inside the Temple, holy place
Serene and wrinkled holy face
Of Anna, without spouse or home,
Resting, praying, rare did roam

But worshiped, singing loud and long
Though weak in age, her voice was strong
Giving thanks and prophecy
To all who would the Savior see.

Not all the passing years would trade
Though petals of a rose will fade,
But perfume lasts to scent the air,
To know I Am, you must declare.

Dear Sister,

Oh, that the fruit of our lips would issue forth a continual praise of Christ! How blessed we would be, for surely we would find ourselves discovering new things to praise him about. His glorious attributes, omnipotence, omniscience, and his unchanging nature constantly astound us. His unfailing love reaches down and touches our lives. His mercies are new every morning, and how we long for them, becoming more and more dependant on his grace to sustain us. Can the depths of God ever be searched out? Shall we not try? A lifetime was not long enough for Anna to sing his praises. Will it be long enough for us? Let us then, with abandonment, praise him with the fruit of our lips. We, the aroma of Christ, must lift up the sacrifice of praise for as long as we have breath. We will never run out of praises, for his glory can be lauded from now until eternity.

A Prayer

Let my life be marked with the praises and declarations of your goodness and love. May my speech be seasoned with salt, let my lips open with the law of kindness. Let my breath be taken to laud your loving kindness and compassion. If you, Lord, will inspire me, I shall not tire of this endless and eternal charge.

A WILD MAN

"He must increase, but I must decrease." John 3:30

"For we know in part and we prophesy in part, but when perfection comes, the imperfect disappears."
1 Corinthians 13:9,10

Leather girdle, hair of length,
A wild man, with wild strength
In Jordan's wilderness he cried
"Repent for the kingdom of God is nigh."

And when he spoke, the way was plain
A crowd did gather, his baptism famed
Thought of as mighty, he spoke with wrath,
Of one whose shoe he dare not latch.

One did appear, he bore witness to,
Then his ministry and time were through.
Like sun that makes the moonlight cease,
To know I Am, you must decrease.

Dear Sister,

We must not place value in our ministries, in our works, in ourselves. John the Baptist wanted to decrease, while Jesus increased. It is the Lord who gives, and the Lord who takes away. If it is no longer I that live, then I shall see more and more of Christ, and less and less of me. We can expect that when the Lord reveals himself, we will be reduced. Like a flame, his message will burn through us, and as it burns it will cleanse out the dross in our own hearts. Doesn't a tall candle shrink as it burns? As we shine, we shall find ourselves diminished. We may be left with little or nothing, but why shall we grieve? Does not our loss cause us to be beautiful in his sight? He is Jehovah Jireh, our provider. No good thing will he withhold from his children. We should not doubt his goodness. The one whose shoe we are unworthy to latch has washed our feet. And how he loves us! What is washed away is but filth and dirt, and we are clean. As we become more like him, we shall desire more of him in us. And then we shall say, "I will be satisfied, when I awake, with his likeness."

A Prayer

Lord, let me decrease that your glory may be seen in all its fullness. Remove from me selfish ambition, vainglory and fear of men. Strip from me the inward parts that hinder others from seeing you in your purity and truth. Let me be a transparent vessel, so you can shine freely in your beauty.

A GIFT

"I tell you the truth," Jesus said to them, " no one who has left home or wife or brothers or parents or children for the sake of the kingdom of God will fail to receive many times as much in this age and, in the age to come, eternal life."
Luke 18:29,30

A crowded table, by men enclosed
Box gripped tight, she would impose
Heart is pounding with strength and force,
A prompting desire, an unaltered course.

Breaking through, she held her breath,
A spikenard spilled to prepare his death,
From his head came forth a scent,
Rare and precious, cost well spent.

They did not understand her act
Her love and motive they did lack,
As alabaster box, now empty and used,
To know I Am, your life you lose.

Dear Sister,

What lessons we can learn from the woman who poured out her valuable offering upon Jesus. What does your life consist of? Possessions? Mary poured out her perfume. Money? The widow gave her last mite. An occupation? Peter left his fishing nets. Christ said we must lose our life to find it again. Our life consists of things that are close to our hearts. Is Christ closer to your heart than these things? Can you lose them, for his sake? We must seek first the kingdom of God, and lay aside every thing that is a weight. When we do, it is a lovely act of worship in our Father's eyes. Christ gave his life as broken bread and poured out wine. He laid aside everything, even his life. It was his love for us which compelled him. What motivates us? He redeemed our soul! Should we not pour out our lives to him in thankful adoration? Let us bring our gifts to him with reckless abandon, knowing he receives them from our hands.

A Prayer

I will bring a gift to the Master. I will bring my life, myself. Help me, Lord to give freely to you, to pour out my offerings to you as Mary did. I want to be generous in my gift. She gave costly perfume. Show me what I can bring to your feet as my acceptable worship. You are worthy.

Linda McGinnis & Diane McGinnis

9
THE FOLLOWERS

"We have left everything to follow you…"
Luke 19:27

IN A CLOUD

*"The man who enters by the gate is the shepherd of his sheep.
The watchman opens the gate for him, and the sheep listen to his
voice. He calls his own sheep by name and leads them out.
When he has brought out all his own, he goes on ahead of them,
and his sheep follow him because they know his voice."*
John 10:2-4

Three men upon a hilltop stood,
Conversing of a higher good
In glory, splendid, spoke of death,
Previewed the destined, dying breath.

And drowsy three lay on the ground
Asleep had fallen, full and sound,
Awoke and in confusion saw
The Master, Moses, Elijah.

One blurted out unknowingly,
We must give honor to these three!
From cloud so bright it covered them,
To know I Am, you must hear Him.

Dear Sister,

What a vision Peter, James and John had on the mountaintop with Jesus. We are told in the Psalms that the voice of the Lord breaks the cedars and strips the forest bare. Then why, oftentimes, is it so hard for us to hear him? We strain our ears and quiet our souls, waiting in expectation. Have we, like the disciples, been lulled to sleep in the interlude? Our eyes drowsy and heavy with need of repose? Let us awaken and open our eyes, seeing clearly enough to give him the honor that is due his name. Though others teach us and give us guidance and encouragement, we have only one Lord and Master. Let us give him our full attention, seeking his voice within us to bear witness to the truths we are hearing with our ears. He is the shepherd who leads us to good pasture, providing the words of eternal life to feed our souls. With the disciples, we will learn to say, "To whom shall we go? For you have the words of eternal life."

A Prayer

I will give you glory and honor. I will not give it to any other. Lord, help me to hear you. Rid all confusion and help me hear the clear sound of your voice. I want to see you high and lifted up, a vision of you as you truly are.

SISTERS

"Every good and perfect gift is from above, coming down from the Father of heavenly lights, who does not change like shifting shadows." James 1:17

"Even as the Son of man came not to be ministered unto, but to minister, and to give his life a ransom for many." Matthew 20:28

Sister Martha, never wrong,
Always confident and strong
She toiled, she spun, she would provide,
Like churning butter, side to side.

Sister Mary, heart of need
As soft as soil prepared for seed,
His words came down like rain in drought
Martha missed them, cumbered about.

Both sisters loved the Savior's face
But Mary chose the better place.
Though Martha's heart desired to please,
To know I Am, you must receive.

Dear Sister,

When we receive something from someone else's hand, we experience a measure of humility. Our need is revealed, and yet met at the same time. There comes a time when we must cease from our own duties, service, and activities. We must put ourselves in a position to receive. Martha was probably comfortable being a busy servant. She was the hostess, and had opened her house in a gift of hospitality. It was her responsibility to care for her guests. But Christ was there! If her heart had acknowledged his ultimate Lordship over both her and her house, she might have sat quietly and listened. His words would have been sufficient for her and her guests. Mary was commended, for the place she chose was at Jesus' feet. What position will we choose? Acknowledge his Lordship, and receive all that he has for you.

A Prayer

Lord, I want to be like Mary. Help me to stop my busy bustling about, caught up in doing all manner of tasks. Instead I would rather "be". It is when I sit quietly at your feet that everything around me falls into place. Priorities and perspective come when I wait in your presence. Open my ears, that I may hear you speak. Let me display humility as I acknowledge your Lordship. The tasks of my hand will not prosper if I do them at the expense of my fellowship with you. Help me seek first your kingdom and lay aside useless activity. Even good activity, if not at your request, will take my eyes off you. I want to be still, and know that you are God.

COME DOWN

"He who has been stealing must steal no longer, but must work, doing something useful with his own hands, that he may have something to share with those in need." Ephesians 4:28

"The thief comes only to steal, kill and destroy; I have come that they may have life, and have it to the full."
John 10:10

A little man, he could not see,
So climbed into the boughs of tree
Craned his neck and stretched his eye
Stepped in branches lifted high,

Unexpected, Jesus spoke
Please come down, his soul awoke
This day I will dine with you,
Resentment filled the crowd anew

This man is a well known cheat
In taxes gathers more than meet
The sick, physician needs to heal,
To know I Am, you must not steal.

Dear Sister,

It is a much better outlook to be ready to give rather than to take. How unexpected for us was the day Jesus called on us to share our lives and resources with others instead of focusing on what we could gather in for ourselves. Such an attitude possessed Zacchaeus when he made the decision to give half his goods to the poor, and to restore fourfold to anyone he had cheated. Zacchaeus had spent his career handling money, counting it up and valuing its worth in an earthly sense. It was a new feeling to be giving it away, thinking of those who were immersed in poverty's grip and caring about those who struggled to make ends meet. We, who have so much in heavenly blessings, should also be ready to see those around us who are in need. To share with them our resources as the Lord leads us. Truly, it is much more blessed to give, whether it be love, time, or earthly goods. Let us give freely and with a ready heart.

A Prayer

Lord, we should not keep all you have given us to ourselves. Let me freely give, as you have given to me. Help me to do it sincerely, and with a ready and joyful heart.

SONS OF THUNDER

"Then he said to them, 'Whoever welcomes this little child in my name welcomes me; and whoever welcomes me welcomes the one who sent me. For he who is the least among you all—
he is the greatest.' "
Luke 9:48

Sons of Thunder, wild and loud,
Who's the greatest in the crowd?
Why do others use your name
To cast out devils? They've no claim!

And how can village turn away
The one who teaches, we'll repay!
Oh, Master, let us call down fire
Burn up all whom we desire!

Master's words are stern and kind
You go astray, your spirit's blind
Take care for little child's face,
To know I Am, you must give grace.

Dear Sister,

How swift the rulers of this world and religious leaders are to exercise their authority, indeed, to revel in it. Jesus was no such example, but came to serve and give his life a ransom for many. Poor James and John received a stern reprimand from Jesus for their attitude of vengeance. And so do we. We are to extend grace to those around us, and let God be the Judge. Let us be the least, the lowest, the servant, the slave. We are to pour out our lives as Jesus did, taking care for the children and the weak. We must put away selfish ambition, along with ungodly desires for respectful greetings in the marketplace and the acclaim of men. We please God by taking on the mantle of humility and wearing it without complaint. Let us walk as Jesus did: gentle, embracing little children, teaching the words of truth, serving those he puts in our path. Let this mind be in you which was in Christ Jesus: a humble, lowly, obedient one which glorifies the Father.

A Prayer

Lord, you have shown us an example of meekness. Let me learn to give grace. Fill me with the Holy Spirit, that I might become gentle, and more like Christ.

THE LAST SUPPER

"They profess that they know God; but in works they deny him, being abominable, and disobedient, and unto every good work reprobate." Titus 1:16

All twelve had gathered round to dine,
He broke the bread, he passed the wine,
His spirit troubled, a somber claim,
A dark revelation, without a name.

Deny the Lord, one of us?
Among the closest ones he trusts?
Yet waiting in the dark, his fate,
Satan huddled, while Judas ate.

Thirty coins in a padded purse
Better not born, than to bear this curse,
Unlike a man who hung and died,
To know I Am, do not deny.

Dear Sister,

There is a sort of denial where we do not confess to know Christ. Peter denied the Lord with his lips three times prior to Christ's death. There is another kind of denial, one where our actions deny the Lord. If we love Christ, our actions and our confessions will speak, confirming this is true. There is a chilling account of how Judas betrayed Christ. This denial led to Judas' death. He banded together with men who thought they could kill Christ. Christ was captured in the garden, but he could have called more that twelve legions of angels to fight on his behalf. He was crucified by men, but only because he was willing to be the sacrificed Lamb. For one who had been a disciple, Judas faced a terrible end to his existence. The story of Peter's denial has quite a different ending. God's forgiveness was there for Peter. Jesus knew Peter, and his weakness, for Christ looks upon the heart. Do we really believe Christ is God? Do we desire to live and profess Christ, but struggle because of weakness and fear? We need the Holy Spirit! See what boldness Peter had after Pentecost! We should live lives that profess Christ, by obedience to his word. We should be willing, when challenged, to profess our love for him. If we struggle with denial, we should ask to be filled with the Holy Spirit. Then we will have the boldness we need to live for him, and speak of Christ to those around us.

A Prayer

Lord, let me not ever betray you. Help my actions to reveal my faith, and let my lips be ready to acknowledge that I know you. Keep me far from men who would wear away my confession. I would confess you until you return, and hear you in turn, confess my name before the Father.

FATEFUL FIRE

"And for this purpose I was appointed a herald and an apostle—I am telling the truth, I am not lying—and a teacher of the true faith to the Gentiles."
1 Timothy 2:7

"Simon, Simon, Satan has asked to sift you as wheat. But I have prayed for you, Simon, that your faith may not fail. And when you have turned back, strengthen your brothers."
Luke 22:31,32

By the warming firelight
A servant saw familiar sight,
And peering with a pointed stare,
You were with him, she declared.

Not I, denial sprung so quick,
And then another conscience prick
You knew him, and were one of his,
Two more accusers added this

And cursing as he did deny
The rooster crowed, he left to cry,
For like a glass reflects a view,
To know I Am, you must be true.

Dear Sister,

There are times in our lives when we, like Peter, fail to speak the truth and confess our relationship to Christ. Fortunately, if we confess our sins he is faithful and just to forgive us, and cleanse us. We still feel sorrow at our weakness. We find ourselves making excuses or downplaying the role Christ has in our lives. We have need of courage to speak the truth. We need to decide to speak in honesty and sincerity no matter the cost. We also need wisdom and discernment, there is a time and a place to plant the seeds of the gospel in the hearts of men. Perhaps Peter feared arrest. Perhaps he forgot that Jesus had a plan for his life, a plan for him to rise up in boldness and lead thousands to a saving knowledge of Christ. There are times when we fall short of what God wants for us, but we can take comfort in the words of our Lord, "I have prayed for you." And then when we have turned back, we can with Peter, strengthen our brothers. No weakness or mistake is too large to be transformed by the grace of God. He is able.

A Prayer

Lord, I want to speak the truth of Christ, and I do not want to shrink back. I wish to declare you are my Lord and Savior to all who surround me. I need you to pray for me, because at times the confession of my lips may not be easy. Give me boldness to open my mouth for your glory.

THE PRISON DOOR

"The Spirit of the Sovereign Lord is on me, because the Lord has anointed me to preach good news to the poor. He has sent me to bind up the brokenhearted, to proclaim freedom for the captives and release for the prisoners."
Isaiah 61:1

Rebellion, crime, arrest as well
A prison yard, a darkened cell,
With rats and moldy crust of bread
In shame he lays his guilty head,

And hears the shouts that would condemn
The Innocent, the God of men
And through a rusted window grate,
He sees the mob so full of hate,

And from their mouths he hears his name
At their request, release obtained
The prison door unlocked with key
To know I Am, you must go free.

Dear Sister,

He led captives in his train, and gave gifts to men! One of the gifts he gives us is freedom. Freedom from our sin, our past, and our guilt. How fitting that at the moment the crowd called for the crucifixion, a guilty captive was released and sent out from the prison cell. Do you think he paused to consider the innocent man who died in his place? We have all sinned and fallen short of his glory, and upon Christ was laid the iniquity of all mankind. Because he took our sin, we no longer bear it, but in repentance let it fall from our weary shoulders. We are free! We don't deserve it, but he gives generously and without reproach. What weight disappears when forgiveness comes, what cleansing and joy in our souls! Let us not take this freedom for granted, but continue to walk in newness of life. After the stench and filth of the prison of our shame, freedom is a welcome and glorious release. Stretch your arms and legs, run and skip like calves in the stall. Shout and rejoice, for freedom has come into your life. He has bought it with his death.

A Prayer

You have taken my place. You have died for me. What gratitude fills my heart! The death that was prepared for me is no longer mine. All that remains is glorious freedom. Thank you for paying the price.

ONE LAST CHANCE

"Then he said, 'Jesus, remember me when you come into your
kingdom.' Jesus answered him, 'I tell you the truth, today you
will be with me in paradise.' "
Luke 23:42,43

Jesus, on the cross, travailing
Thieves on either side, assailing
Hurling insults, one prevailed
If you're the Christ, then loose our nails

The other, softer, gave rebuke
We have earned death absolute,
This man did commit no crime
His innocence is pure, divine.

With obeisance, he spoke his name,
Jesus, Lord, I share your pain,
Remember me, forgive my sin,
To know I Am, you trust in Him.

Dear Sister,

What hope is ours when we think of the confession of
the thief on the cross! Surely his example can leave no doubt
that a life of good works is not necessary to live eternally in
paradise. As one who was paying the penalty for crimes he had
committed, and recognizing his punishment was just, he was
still able to see the salvation offered to him in Christ. He took
upon himself the promise of eternity. It is never too late, we are
never too old or too sinful to be beyond the saving grace of our
Lord. What mercy from on high is revealed in the response of
Jesus to this man who had lived a lawless life. There was instant
healing and remedy for the burden of his guilt and sorrow. Let
us remember that no sinner is beyond the touch of God. All
men deserve an opportunity to hear of the forgiving mercy of
Jesus. Let God be the judge, since it is he who chooses to
deliver men from eternal punishment. Let us revel in such
amazing grace, dispensed at moments which determine a man's
destiny after death. His hand is mighty to save.

A Prayer

In you is the way to eternal life. I trust in your mercy and grace.
Lord, I stand in awe of your love toward men. It is so pure and
heavenly! May many reach out and touch this grace, even in
their final hour.

THE LINEN SHROUD

"Now Joseph was a disciple of Jesus, but secretly because he feared the Jews. With Pilate's permission he came and took the body." John 19:38

"Nicodemus brought a mixture of myrrh and aloes, about seventy five pounds. Taking Jesus body, the two of them wrapped it, with the spices, in strips of linen."
John 19:39,40

Dusk approached, Golgotha still
A council member scanned the hill
To take a stand against the mob,
He sought the kingdom realm of God,

To Pilate he made bold request,
To care for bruised King, holiest
Removed the body, sadly bowed
And wrapped it in a linen shroud

Carried gently, placed in room
An empty cave, a ready tomb
Majestic triumph, dying breath,
To know I Am, embrace his death.

Dear Sister,

Think of the quiet night when this noble deed was
accomplished. Two men, who up until this time had feared
being known publicly as disciples of Christ, now stepped boldly
to the cross and gently took down his body. How reverent and
careful they laid him out, preparing him in the proper custom
for burial. With pounds and pounds of ointment and spice they
saturated the linen sheets as they wrapped his lifeless form.
What thoughts passed through their mind during the stillness
of the night? What a sweet fragrance filled the air as they
worked, clung to their hands and clothing, would ever be a
reminder to them of all Jesus said and did! Did they wonder at
the culmination of Jesus life, a dark day and a violent death?
Did hope even then, fill their hearts as they embraced him,
taking him to the garden where the empty tomb was waiting?
Let us, as these two disciples did, embrace his death, knowing
that so much was accomplished for our salvation. "Let us also
go, that we may die with him!" As Thomas said in impulse, let
us say in earnest, with full knowledge that to live is Christ, and
to die is gain.

A Prayer

Lord, I will ponder your death and burial. In your death, there
is a sweet savor, a beautiful fragrance of sacrifice, and of love. I
know as I think of this event, I will walk away with the
lingering scent of the most precious of ointments.

TOUCH ME

"He said to them, 'Why are you troubled, and why do doubts rise in your minds? Look at my hands and my feet. It is I myself! Touch me and see; a ghost does not have flesh and bones, as you see I have.' " Luke 24:38,39

Missing out on visit sweet,
"He was with us," friends repeat
But doubtful of the Father's plan,
And questioning the Son of man,

Unless with mine own hand to feel
The place the soldier scarred with zeal
And into side that pierced did flow,
With blood and water, I don't know.

Put your finger here, said He,
Loose the doubts that bother thee,
For like the wind that changes course,
To know I Am, you touch the source.

Dear Sister,

How stubborn Thomas must have seemed to the disciples as they tried to convince him they had seen the Lord! They were sure, but Thomas needed to see for himself. What a blessing he is to us, an example of someone who won't take another's word for the presence of Christ, but must see it with his own eyes. Indeed, he was present the next time Jesus appeared to his disciples, and encouraged by the Lord himself to touch the scars on his hands and side. His response, "My Lord and My God," he declared with fervor. The Lord says we who have not seen and yet believe, are blessed. Further than this, we have access now to the throne of grace. Each one of us as an individual is able to touch the source, to kneel at his feet, to have an intimate relationship with him. Let us not be satisfied with the reports of others, but press in to the Holy of Holies for ourselves, and touch the source of our salvation with our own hands. He is waiting.

A Prayer

Lord, even now I long to touch you. Sometimes my faith is weak, and I need to touch you so that you may revive it again. As I come, may you dispel all my doubts!

10
PARABLES

"I will open my mouth in parables…"
Psalm 78:2

JUSTIFIED

"Has not my hand made all these things, and so they came into being?" declares the Lord. "This is the one I esteem: he who is humble and contrite in spirit, and trembles at my word."
Isaiah 66:2

"Humble yourselves, therefore, under God's mighty hand, that he may lift you up in due time."
1 Peter 5:6

Two men in the Temple, praying,
One so upright, virtues saying
I am not in sin, he stands,
A cheat, corrupt, with wicked hands,

But the other, on his face
Beat his chest, was low and base
God show mercy, let it fall
Change my heart, and hear my call

One man went back home the same
One man was released from shame
Which of these does your prayer show?
To know I Am, you must bow low.

Dear Sister,

Let us examine our prayers regarding those who are lost in sin around us. Do we thank God we are not like them, seeped in vile, ungodly practices and caught in the chains of wickedness? But for the grace of God we would be right there with them! Do we recognize the keeping power of God's hand in our lives? It is he who keeps us from falling and shows us the way to walk. With a humble and contrite heart, we will not be refused at the throne. Indeed, he draws near to those who bow low, seeking him in his beauty and sovereignty. He draws near to those who acknowledge the world is his, and recognize he has the authority to do as he pleases. This is the God we serve, the one who is Lord over us, and we fear and reverence him as we pray. It is with great joy and pleasure that God raises the humble soul, exalting him to a place of honor that he did not seek for himself. Choose to sit in the low place, and be taken up by the careful hands of Almighty God.

A Prayer

Lord, I cannot claim any righteousness for myself. I come humbly, and I bow low. I am not worthy, yet I know you are rich in grace and mercy. May I receive these from your hand.

TWO MEN

"All they asked was that we should continue to remember the poor, the very thing I was eager to do." Galatians 2:10

"Repent, then and turn to God, so that your sins may be wiped out, that times of refreshing may come from the Lord, and that he may send the Christ who has been appointed for you—even Jesus." Acts 3:19,20

Dressed in purple, linen fine
Servants, money, food and wine
While the beggar on the street
Covered with sores and longed to eat

He died and angels bore him far
To comfort him and heal all scars
But rich man in the hell of fire,
Longed for water, need was dire.

No, the one of old replied,
For good was yours before you died,
Like evening when the light is spent,
To know I Am, you must repent.

Dear Sister,

How we long for the times of refreshing to come! How we sympathize with the man who was so wrapped up in his own life of luxury that he forgot to help the beggar in need at his doorstep. We thirst with him when we think of being denied a drink of water in the wasteland of hell. How much better it is to give from our surplus of material and spiritual goods, showing by our deeds that we do not consider earth our home. We must recognize that all we have has been given to us from God's hand. Let us repent now, of the selfishness in our lives that keeps another from dwelling in God's blessings. Who is at your doorstep today, in need of food, comfort or love? In all your abundance and luxury, will you minister to him? Let the times of refreshing in God's presence wash over you and those you love and comfort in Jesus' name. Such is the ministry of those who love him.

A Prayer

Lord, I despise my own selfishness. I ask that you help me give to all those who are in need around me. I want to remember in this life how to minister to those who are without earthly comforts. Father, give me compassion.

THE NARROW DOOR

"A certain man was preparing a great banquet and invited many guests. At the time of the banquet he sent his servants to tell those who had been invited, 'Come, for everything is now ready.' " Luke 14:16

"Then the angel said to me, 'Write: Blessed are those who are invited to the wedding supper of the Lamb!' " Revelation 19:9

A narrow door is open now,
To enter in, you must know how
For shut and locked it soon will be
And though you knock, there is no key

And plead, the head of house won't yield
I know you not, the door is sealed
You can't come in with guilty hearts,
So go away, you must depart

Great weeping of the soul, abased,
As all the chosen find their place
Like honored guest, invited friend,
To know I Am, you must come in.

Dear Sister,

How simple the path to salvation, to God himself!
Enter in, he welcomes us. He invites us into his kingdom with
open arms. What is required? To come through the door of
repentance and join the multitude of guests for the wedding
feast. The secret is, you must do it now! Today is the day of
salvation, the time you hear his voice is the time to act and
obey. We have no certainty of tomorrow, no way of knowing if
another opportunity will come. There is something very
exciting about coming into the kingdom. It is as if you have
fallen off a precipice of the known into the realm of the
unknown and unfamiliar. Each man must make the choice, and
though we tell others of the wedding feast, they must make the
choice on their own to come in and join the multitude. There is
no-one who can say he wasn't invited. Even the poor, the sick,
the lame, and those in the highways and byways have been
called. Let us join in sending out the invitation, let us enter in
ourselves to the abundant life of the kingdom. The feast awaits!

A Prayer

Lord, you truly are the way. I must help in declaring your broad
invitation! Help me to let others know that the day of their
salvation is today.

THE LOST SHEEP

"For the Son of Man came to seek and save what was lost."
Luke 19:10

"Then he calls his friends and neighbors together and says,
Rejoice with me; I have found my lost sheep."
Luke 15:6

A sheep was lonely on a hill
Lost from herd and wandering, ill
His ragged coat was full of burrs
He stumbled, all his steps unsure

And in the storm of rain and wind
He pressed into a rocky bend
To wait and hope for brighter day
In morning try to find his way

But in the night a voice did cry
And shepherd found him safe and dry
Like hunter traces path with hound,
To know I Am, you must be found.

Dear Sister,

How forlorn we feel when we stray from the safety of the fold. We wander about on our own, fighting obstacles with every step! Our energy is sapped, our heart is lonely for our brethren, and we collect the signs of our abandonment: burrs, dirt and mud. With stumbling steps we try for our destination, often becoming injured in the process. Thank God for his unceasing persistence. There is no hill or valley that is out of his sight, no cave or hiding place beyond his range of vision. No inclement weather could delay his search, no injury he finds is past healing. No amount of dirt and muck repulses him, for he is able to bear us up in his arms, and has with him the means to restoration. With the same love that he extends to us, he also reaches for other wayward sheep, those among us who perhaps have lost the way. What relief and comfort it is that we don't have to shepherd ourselves. Let the Good Shepherd care for you. Resist him not as he returns you to a place a safety and green pasture. You have need of his care.

A Prayer

Lord, I accept your love. Be my shepherd, guide me and care for me. If I lose my way, seek me out and help me to return.

A RARE PRIZE

"If you call out for insight and cry aloud for understanding, and if you look for it as for silver and search for it as for hidden treasure, then you will understand the fear of the Lord, and find the knowledge of God."
Proverbs 2:3-5

Treasure buried in a field
Hid again, its place is sealed,
Then to sell all earthly goods,
To buy the ground it's in, he would.

Merchant searching for fine pearls
Diving long, the shell unfurls
One of beauty, rare is shown,
Discovered now, he sells to own.

Find the treasure, hide it well,
To own it, all your goods do sell
Like priceless pearl, desired prize,
To know I Am, you must be wise.

Dear Sister,

What diligence is needed as we search out the treasures of God! We are encouraged to call out and cry aloud in our pursuits for heavenly wisdom. A valuable and lasting treasure we seek, one that cannot be corrupted by the decay of this earth, or stolen by thieves. There is something we give up in the search, for in searching we remove ourselves from the pursuit of material and earthly goods. A wonderful day it is for us, when we find out that Jesus Christ is made unto us wisdom from God! In him are hidden all the treasures of wisdom and knowledge. In seeking him, we find the pearl of great price, the storehouse of mysteries beyond our imagination. In knowing him, we become wise beyond our capabilities. Time spent in the pursuit of God is never wasted or spent in vain. For us, not only do we seek, but keep seeking, until the answers to the questions in our hearts appear. The treasure is there, it is buried. Don't give up in your search for truth. It is a worthwhile enterprise.

A Prayer

Lord, you are so valuable to me. I desire you much more than ready earthly treasures. If I seek with a sincere heart, the treasure will be found. Father, help me to see the truth.

A FATHER'S LOVE

"As a shepherd seeketh out his flock in the day that he is among his sheep that are scattered; so will I seek out my sheep, and will deliver them out of all places where they have been scattered in the cloudy and dark day."
Ezekiel 34:12

Eager son, so young and free
Spent his portion the world to see.
Sin for a season was pleasant and fine,
But ended a servant, eating with swine.

Dirty, hungry, mired in mud,
He came to his senses and in a flood,
Of reason remembered his Father and home,
The comfort and love, he had once known.

The Father, elated, his son was not dead,
Showered great favor upon his head,
Like shepherd for lost sheep would yearn,
To know I Am, you must return.

Dear Sister,

All we like sheep have gone astray. Even when we wander, doesn't he continue to be the Good Shepherd? He doesn't forget us, he searches us out. We cannot lose our place in the flock of the Lord, for no one can snatch us out of his hand. Let us be reassured, fleshy desires can cause us to seek out a better pasture, but we cannot undo our Shepherd's heart. It is agape that is bestowed on us, from God himself, and his love does not rest on our faithfulness. Our Lord explains his loving heart in a parable of a father and a wayward son. Though the son leaves his father, he can no more become fatherless than a sheep can become shepherd-less. The son doubts his worthiness upon his return to his father, but finds his worthiness is irrelevant. He is still treated as a son, and given much love. As a father pities his children, so the Lord pities us. Return, return, you shall be met with love. You are still his child, carved on the palm of his hand. You are still the apple of his eye. His love for you is greater than you, it is never diminished. Everlasting and irrevocable, it is as immutable as he is himself. As the star shone on a long ago night over Bethlehem, let the shining light of his love lead you home.

A Prayer

Lord, thank you for your great searching, relentless love. It not only sought me out in my despair, but lifted me up out of the mire and set my feet upon a rock. Your Father's heart leaves me speechless and in awe. Such forgiveness, such undeserved grace! Despite my unworthy state, you have made me a son, and treated me with favor. I will thank you and bless your name as long as I live. My heart clings to you.

LAMPS THAT LIGHT

*"You prepare a table before me in the presence of my enemies.
You anoint my head with oil; my cup overflows. Surely goodness
and love will follow me all the days of my life, and I will dwell
in the house of the Lord forever."*
Psalm 23:5,6

Lamps at night, in dark and black
Some hold oil, some do lack
Sitting on the sill in wait
For an event, a twist of fate.

Just then a noise, a blasting trump
The virgins from their beds do jump
They run to take their lamps in haste
And then, to meet the groom, they'll race.

Alas, there's five who have no oil
Their future and their plans were spoiled.
Though five were wise, they could not share,
To know I Am, you must prepare.

Dear Sister,

What good is a lamp with no oil? No good at all. The foolish virgins looked prepared. After all, they had a lamp, too. When the telling moment came, their foolishness was discovered. They had an opportunity to prepare their lamps with oil, and neglected to do it. Perhaps other chores seemed more important. They might have thought the call would come by day, and they would not need oil after all. Perhaps they had just assumed the other virgins would provide them with the necessary oil. In any case, they were wrong. What good is our religion without the oil of the Holy Spirit? To some, those with empty religion look spiritually prepared. They look like they are wise, for they have a lamp, too. We need the Holy Spirit in our lives, so we will be prepared to join Jesus, the bridegroom. We need to make sure of our readiness, and not make the mistake of the foolish virgins. We cannot receive this oil from another person. We have to go to the Lord ourselves, and ask him to fill our lamp. Then we can rejoice, and our hearts will overflow with peace. Our lives will be marked with the wisdom, comfort, and power of the Holy Spirit of God. We can ask him to fill us at any time. Then, when unexpected challenges arise, we will be ready. In the most telling moment of all, the arrival of the bridegroom, we will be found with a ready lamp.

A Prayer

Lord, fill my lamp with oil. Then whether I wake or sleep, I will have peace, knowing that I am prepared for your coming. I can depend on no other for my supply of oil, but I come to you in supplication. Anoint my head with oil, pour it over me, let it run down my face and cover my garments. I need the oil of joy, and a lamp that is full!

PLOW AND PLANT

"Remember this: Whoever sows sparingly will also reap sparingly, and whoever sows generously will also reap generously." 2 Corinthians 9:6

"Now he who supplies seed to the sower and bread for food will also supply and increase your store of seed and will enlarge the harvest of your righteousness."
2 Corinthians 9:10

Sower worked in furrowed field
Oxen, plough, and strength to wield
Seed cupped in a hopeful hand
With a prayer he sowed the land.

Some fell on a trampled path
Eaten by the birds so fast
Some on rocks that held no dew
Some where thorns and thistles grew

But most fell on the choicest ground
Soil where the rain came down.
For harvest of abundant crops
To know I Am, you plant a lot.

Dear Sister,

Plant and plant, and then when you're feeling weary, plant some more. What kind of harvest do you want to see? A bountiful one for God's glory? Scatter the seed God has given you, depend on him to increase it if stores run low. Seeds of love, joy and peace are shed abroad from our hearts, and with the leading of the Holy Spirit they find the ready ground where they can grow. Perhaps it's the plow you're wrestling with, digging up the hard soil in preparation for the planting time. The hot sun beats down on your back, and the sweat is running freely. Don't give up, each phase of the work must be done thoroughly for the abundant harvest to follow. Don't cut corners, or the crop will suffer, not having the required elements to flourish. God brings the rain. It is the Lord who causes the seed to grow in its proper time. Is your seed pouch full from last year's harvest? Disperse the contents into the ready soil of the garden of men's souls. It is a gift you can share, knowing the reward will be soon to follow, a harvest of righteousness that will be a blessing to you in days to come.

A Prayer

Lord, I know you can bring an increase, if I am faithful to plow and plant. There is work to be done. What an honor it is for me to share in this righteous labor! Let me sow patiently, and see all that you bring forth as a result.

BLEEDING MAN

"Suppose a brother or sister is without clothes and daily food. If one of you says to him, "Go, I wish you well; keep warm and well fed," but does nothing about his physical needs, what good is it?" James 2:15,16

"For anyone who does not love his brother, whom he has seen, cannot love God, whom he has not seen."
1 John 4:20

On a trip to Jericho,
Misfortune came in form of foe,
So beaten, stripped, and robbed of coins,
He lay despairing, bleeding loins.

And then in pity, neighbor passed,
And knelt beside the wounded mass
With bandage, salve and medicine
And words of comfort aided him.

And for the healing at the inn,
This neighbor paid the bill again
Restored to health a man can live
To know I Am, you too must give.

Dear Sister,

How many times on the journey of life do we end up just like the bleeding man? Due to circumstances, or the vagaries of living in this unpredictable world, we find ourselves the recipients of injuries and hurts. Perhaps they are injuries to our emotions, our feelings, or our hearts, which are nonetheless as painful as physical wounds. Even our brothers and sisters in the faith, due to misunderstandings and conflicts, can be the vessels through which bruises and mistreatment come. How will we rise above this dilemma? We must be vessels of healing to one another. We must apply with liberality the salve of the healing word of God. We must lift one another in prayer, asking for the sufficient grace of God to be with the one who is suffering. We must be sensitive, and willing to walk those in need to the place where restoration can be obtained. The cost is ours to bear, as the good neighbor in this parable shows us. Let us do to one another as this man has done. With the same comfort you have received, comfort others.

A Prayer

Lord, show me how to minister to he hurting ones around me. Help me to crouch down in compassion, and liberally apply the healing salve. You are always willing to aid the wounded. May I be ready to do the same.

THE BANQUET

"Now it is God who makes both us and you stand firm in Christ. He anointed us, and put his Spirit in our hearts as a deposit, guaranteeing what is to come."
2 Corinthians 1:21,22

A bride adorned in wedding white
Longing for her wedding night
Hand in hand, and heart in heart,
The two will join, never to part

A time engaged, they made their vow
With ring and promise, pledged 'til now
The present, what they knew would come
A day the union would be done.

A banner of love, a table of wine
All prepared for a perfect time
Like fruit with rind, seals and protects,
To know I Am, you must expect.

Dear Sister,

Certainly we have great expectation for the wedding banquet we shall enjoy in heaven. We are promised to Christ and we are his! We are marked with the indwelling of the Holy Spirit of God. We can look forward to the wedding supper of the Lamb, for we are his bride. Just as a man presents a woman with a ring and a promise on their engagement, Christ presents us with the Holy Spirit to keep us until the marriage supper. We should prepare our hearts for him. As we think upon the one we love, our desire to keep ourselves for him alone will grow strong. We know his earnest pledge was given in the gift of the Holy Ghost, and we can be sure that his word will be honored. His word declares we shall be a bride without spot or wrinkle. Let us have expectation in our hearts, as we wait in joyful anticipation. The day of our banquet approaches!

A Prayer

Lord, I will keep myself for you, and wait in hope for the wedding day. How my heart thrills to know you have promised yourself to me, to be a husband for eternity. Such great love you have given to us! I am overwhelmed and full of thankfulness. I will put on the spotless garment you have given, and wear it with an expectation of the marriage supper that is to come.

11
MIRACLES

"I have shown you many great miracles…"
John 10:32

A NEW VESSEL

"You, dear children, are from God, and have overcome them, because the one who is in you is greater than the one who is in the world." 1 John 4:4

"It is for freedom that Christ has set us free." Galatians 5:1

Amongst a crowd so loud it swelled
An only son, by father held
Was seized by demon in a grip
He screamed, and foamed, and himself hit

Disciples tried to cast it out
But in convulsions boy cried out
Upon the ground to writhe and moan
While father watched, his heart undone

Then Jesus drawing near him said,
"Come out," and from this vessel fled
The horror, like a leech would bleed
To know I Am, you must be freed.

Dear Sister,

What compassion fills our heart for the father and son, who lived with this torment in their home and life. What terror for a child to be seized in the grip of the enemy, helpless to free himself. What power in the Christ, who came to set all men free! He is the deliverer. Just as the people of God in Egypt needed Moses to intervene on their behalf, so also we need the deliverer to command the enemy to let go of the souls of men. Jesus is the mediator, the one who is in constant intercession on our behalf. With a word from his gracious lips, the evil departs and is gone forever. What rejoicing fills heaven when a soul is freed! This is the work Christ came to do, to bring deliverance to the captives and freedom to those who are bound. Let us look with merciful eyes at the bondage of men, seeing an opportunity to enter into the work of heaven. Let us bring them to Jesus, the Deliverer, and he will set them free.

A Prayer

Jesus, only you can save these tormented souls. Only you have the power to deliver, the power to free from bondage. I ask that you speak the word on behalf of those who are bound, that they might enter into salvation.

A THANKFUL HEART

"I also assigned two large choirs to give thanks."
Nehemiah 12:31

"Let the word of Christ dwell in you richly as you teach and admonish one another with all wisdom, and as you sing psalms, hymns and spiritual songs with gratitude in your hearts to God." Colossians 3:16

Ten lepers on the edge of town
From a distance, looking on
Eyes of grief, and hearts downcast
Bandaged limbs, and joy long past

Calling out to stop the man
Who filled with mercy, understands
He sent them to the village priest
To show their skin, infection ceased

Amazement filled one joyful soul
And running back, fell worshipful
Expressed his gratitude with vim
To know I Am, you must thank Him.

Dear Sister,

How is it nine restored lepers neglected to thank the
one who healed them? What lapse in manners to say the least, a
travesty when the severity of their sickness is considered.
Physical infirmities that rob us of our abilities are some of the
heaviest crosses to bear in this life. Imagine the hopelessness of
finding oneself in such a condition, where no cure is available,
no remedy yet discovered. Even in our present day we have
diseases such as leprosy, illnesses that cause the sufferer to be
shunned and avoided due to fear of contagion. But Jesus had
something to give these joyless souls, a gift of healing that
would change the course of their lives, bringing them back to
their families and loved ones. Let us have mercy on the sick, on
their cheerless lives, and bring the hope of Jesus' touch to their
hearts. Do you know someone in this condition? Visit him and
share his burden! Oh, pray that the power of God be poured
out to heal the many sick and infirm of the earth!

A Prayer

Jesus, there are many who need your healing touch. I thank you
for pouring out your mercy on the sick. I thank you that your
power to heal is working among men today. Give us thankful
hearts, for your goodness is so great!

THE BENT WOMAN

"I have seen his ways, but I will heal him; I will guide him and restore comfort to him, creating praise on the lips of the mourners in Israel. Peace, peace to those far and near," says the Lord. "And I will heal them."
Isaiah 57:19

One Sabbath day, the Master taught,
When from the corner, bent, distraught
For eighteen long and heavy years,
A woman crouched and shed her tears.

She could not stand and lift her head,
So humbled, wished that she were dead,
Until someone who had the power,
Noticed her and how she cowered.

Touching her, the spine went straight
And Temple leader did berate,
Like tended wound from scar to weal,
To know I Am, you must be healed.

Dear Sister,

What a heavy burden our sins and sorrow lay upon our backs! Bent over with pain and agony, we try to live our lives, until someone tells us the good news, and we find Jesus relieving our shoulders of the weight of our sins. What freedom and joy is ours when we stretch our backs for the first time, free from the binding weights and bondage we have carried. We can raise our head, but our neck is not held upright by pride, it is straightened and supported by the truth and love of God. He tells us his yoke is easy, and his burdens are not grievous. How contrary to the weights of the world that are waiting for a back to climb on. We are instructed to stand firm in our freedom, to lay aside every weight that hinders us in our walk with God. This woman came to the Temple daily, yet found no relief from her infirmity. God forbid that there be those among us who devote their lives to God and never hear of the deliverance and healing power of the Savior. He is ready to take those pains and sorrows. He bore them on his cross, and carried them so that we might be spared. Let go of your wearying burdens today. There is no need to keep them in the presence of his glory.

A Prayer

Lord, you came to heal, to restore, to make straight that which is crooked. Let us pray for the sick as you have instructed. Let us cease not in lifting up their needs, for you are able to heal.

BROKEN CHAINS

"O Lord, truly I am your servant; I am your servant, the son of your maidservant; you have freed me from my chains."
Psalm 116:16
"I will walk about in freedom, for I have sought out your precepts." Psalm 119:45

Sixteen men, the chamber full
Guarding one lone disciple
Before the trial, in the night
He slept between two soldiers tight.

All at once a glow arrived
Woke the man and shook his side,
Chains fell off and he got dressed
Wrapped his cloak and followed, blessed.

The iron gate had opened wide,
The angel guided him outside.
Like eyes of faith can't be explained,
To know I Am, be free from chains.

Dear Sister,

As we follow Christ, there will be times the world will attempt to put us in chains to silence our message. They would "arrest" us, intimidate us, and try to stop our mouths from declaring the good news. Peter had been preaching the gospel with boldness when he found himself cast into prison. It is when we are directly in the center of God's will and plan that the enemy will try to come against us. Not only were there four squads of four soldiers each guarding Peter, but two of the soldiers slept on either side of him. As if that was not enough, he was bound with chains. Even these forbidding obstacles did not stand in the way of God's plan. Our God loves to do the impossible. In our lives, the power and might of the Lord will free us from the hindrances the world tries to lay on us. As believers, we are to walk about in freedom and liberty. In the night, the chains were broken, and Peter went free. Let us also rise up in the night, allowing the chains of intimidation and fear to fall from our bodies. Let us leave the prison cell and find a new and exhilarating walk of freedom, freedom to speak the name of Christ without fear.

A Prayer

Your deliverance is mighty. You are able to grant us a way out of the bondage men try to force on us. Let us give you the glory and walk on in freedom, declaring your greatness.

Linda McGinnis & Diane McGinnis

12
THE MASTER

"For you have only one Master…"

Matthew 23:8

A CARPENTER

"Then he went down to Nazareth with them and was obedient to them. But his mother treasured all these things in her heart. And Jesus grew in wisdom and stature, and in favor with both God and man." Luke 2:51,52

Working at his Father's bench
Hammer, tools and chisel clenched
Growing taller, growing wise,
Learning skill, of craft apprised

Gaining muscle, bearing loads
Hard instruction, words like goads
Nails to pound and job to do,
Favor gathered when it's through

Trade of family passing on,
Polished wood, obedient son
As books give wisdom page by page,
To know I Am, you grow with age.

Dear Sister,

Imagine the outcry of the people from the home town where Jesus grew up. "Isn't this the carpenter," they asked? They couldn't understand where he had obtained such wisdom as he taught in the synagogue. They found it hard to believe he performed miracles. He was only a carpenter in their eyes, in spite of the evidence before them that he was much, much more. What is he to us? A carpenter who builds with wood and tools? Indeed, he is the Master carpenter, who builds our lives and shapes us, making us into a vessel worthy to bear the name of Christ. A builder of men's lives, and with the blueprints to guide him! For as the psalm says, our days were written in his book, before even one of them came to be. How comforting to us, to know he builds according to a plan, and not in a random, haphazard way. How little we now resemble the finished piece, but we have the assurance, the confidence, that he who has begun a good work in us will complete it until the day of Jesus Christ. Hammering, sanding, adding to, and cutting away from our minds and hearts, he works on us. He works until we begin to reveal the beautiful person he made us to be. We can rejoice! We are the work of his hands.

A Prayer

Jesus, I praise you, for you show such patience as you build. I know that you are making me. What a comforting thought. I rest in the knowledge that you have all the wisdom you need to shape and build my life.

THE WAY

"I tell you the truth, unless a kernel a wheat falls to the ground and dies, it remains only a single seed. But if it dies, it produces many seeds." John 12:24

"Now if we died with Christ, we believe that we will also live with him." Romans 6:8

Darkness fell upon the earth
Sun was hidden, light dispersed
Hanging body, load of sin
Will of Father, cup so grim,

He sipped a sponge of spoiled wine,
Above his head a telling sign.
Disciples, friends and women grieved
He bore our pain and agony

The Temple veil was torn in half,
A gift from heaven, open path
With voice that echoed, spirit left,
To know I Am, you yield to death.

Dear Sister,

It must have been a hard thing for the disciples to watch Jesus die. The loss was probably written on their faces, bewilderment and turmoil must have filled their minds. It was the risen Christ himself who had to explain the necessity of his death as the fulfillment of the scriptures- to the disciples on the road to Emmaus. He was opening a way to heaven, a path to the throne of the Father. We also, must die to ourselves in order to live with Christ. He asks us to do no less than he himself has done. Will you drink the cup of the Father's will and lay down your life at his feet? When you give yourself to him in this way, you are not only dead, but your life is hid with Christ in God. What safety and security is ours when we yield to this type of death, counting everything a loss compared to the surpassing greatness of knowing Christ. We die not to be deprived of ourselves, but so the real man can emerge, finding refuge in the Holy of Holies. It is new life and peace, fruit and fruition that comes when we die to self. Let the old nature be crucified with Christ, and rise up in the newness of life he promises to give to those who die with him.

A Prayer

There is a way to new life. I must die to self and be hid with Christ in God. Father, I want to die to self, but you know how I struggle. Hear my prayer. I need you to encourage and help me as I lay down my life.

A COVERING

"For as many of you as have been baptized into Christ have put on Christ." Galatians 3:27

"I delight greatly in the Lord; my soul rejoices in my God. For he has clothed me with garments of salvation, and arrayed me in a robe of righteousness."
Isaiah 61:10

A sinner's cross, a crown of thorns
His back of flesh all ripped and torn
A shouting crowd cried "Crucify!"
His body bruised, a spear in side,

Sin hung rudely on a tree
An act to set all sinners free
The Son of God who loved forgave
And He is risen from the grave!

He died alone, His body bare,
To give us righteous robes to wear
Like coat of skin, slain with a price,
To know I Am, you put on Christ.

Dear Sister,

When we approach the cross of Christ, doesn't the conviction overwhelm us? Our "fig leaves" become all too apparent. Our cover-ups and our attempts to look good before God are rendered useless. Our leaves are shed at the foot of the cross. Then naked and ashamed, we face God. He has provided a garment for us! Put on Christ, be able to receive his greatest provision. Does it not follow that He who clothes the lilies of the field can cause us to have beauty greater than that of King Solomon?

A Prayer

I will put on Christ. Clothe me with Your beauty, instead of any rich garment of this earth. I don't want the fig leaves, or my own righteousness. Will you give me beauty for ashes, and clothes befitting a bride? I will not refuse the covering you have provided for the rudeness of my sin. I will wear it gladly.

LIFE

"Jesus said to her, 'I am the resurrection and the life. He who believes in me will live, even though he dies; and whoever lives and believes in me will never die. Do you believe this?' "
John 11:25,26

Inside the grave, the darkness deep
Lies now a Savior, death can't keep
Without blemish, without stain,
The Father's power soon will reign.

First a silence, then a sound
The Living Word does now surround,
And speaks of life, redemption knows,
A blinding flash, his body rose.

This salvation of perfect design
Happened in one place and time,
Bow down, and worship at his throne,
To know I Am, know Him alone.

Dear Sister,

Think of the awesome power of God revealed at the resurrection! Inside the dark place of death, the lonely tomb, a power greater than death was manifested. Imagine the burst of divine strength and energy that came upon Christ, waking him from the sleep of death. We stand in awe of such an incredible event. For us, death has been swallowed up in victory, its chains can no longer hold us in the grave. Let us meditate on the omnipotence of the Godhead. Such matchless might, such supreme authority as no earthly human has or ever will possess. This knowledge is beyond us, and yet we strive to find him, to know him evermore. What glimpses of divine majesty are laid out for mankind to witness! The Living Word, the Christ, the Spirit eternal teaches and guides us to more of the truth, to more of God himself. Let us press on to know the one eternal, immortal, invisible, and yet accessible to us through the death and resurrection of our Savior Jesus Christ. Let us worship our incredible and magnificent Lord.

A Prayer

Jesus, lead me to all truth. I want to know you, open my eyes. You have set the world before us, distractions and earthly pleasures abound, but in you is life, and in you we can have life more abundantly. Help me set my eyes on you and your kingdom. In you I can hope and wait for eternal life.

A GREAT DAY

"For now we see through a glass darkly; but then face to face: now I know in part; but then shall I know even as also I am known." 1 Corinthians 13:12

"For the Lord himself shall descend from heaven with a shout, with the voice of the archangel, and with the trump of God: and the dead in Christ shall rise first; Then we which are alive and remain shall be caught up together with them in the clouds to meet the Lord in the air: and so shall we ever be with the Lord." 1 Thessalonians 4:16,17

Like lightning shining east to west,
The Son of man returning, dressed
In glory, majesty and power
For the awesome final hour.

Carcass, eagles eating flesh,
Sun and moon and stars distressed,
Falling, failing, mourning men,
The day will come, awaited end.

No man knows the day or hour
The Son of Man will come in power.
And for that day creation groans,
To know I Am, as we are known.

Dear Sister,

The final day for all men awaits. Christ will come again in glory and in power. We have a great hope in this day. It is not surprising that we long for it, even creation groans for its full redemption. Even though we have peace and joy in Christ in this life, we live in a fallen world. We see sin, sorrow, and sickness. We can only imagine the beauty, goodness, and splendor that Adam and Eve enjoyed before the fall. The end of the age will come, and Christ will reclaim the earth. All shall be made right. We long for this day. When we reign with Christ, we will know him as we are known. Now we see him through a glass darkly. We shall see him face to face. These afflictions we suffer are light and temporary when compared with eternal glory. Some of us will die and enter glory, others will be caught up in the air and taken to heaven. We should comfort one another with the hope of his return. When he says, "Surely, I come quickly," our heart responds! Our spirit exclaims, "Even so, come Lord Jesus!"

A Prayer

Lord, I await your coming with fervent hope! My ear is listening for the trumpet sound, the voice of the angel, the announcement of your long awaited return. My eye is looking for the shining of your glory in the clouds, the splendor of which we have never seen before. Your splendor will blind us in its beauty, for we will see you as you are.

13297462R00113

Made in the USA
Charleston, SC
29 June 2012